December 2

To Patrick

With all best wishes,

Vanessa.

INSIDE OUT

A LIFE IN STAGES

Vanessa Rosenthal

Red Door

Published by RedDoor
www.reddoorpress.co.uk

The author and publisher gratefully acknowledge permissions granted to reproduce the copyright material in this book. Every effort has been made to trace copyright holders and to obtain their permission for the use of copyright material. The publisher apologises for any errors or omissions in the above list and would be grateful if notified of any corrections that should be incorporated in future reprints or editions of this book

Extract on page 175 and p.178 from 'Fern Hill' by Dylan Thomas. Taken from *The Collected Poems of Dylan Thomas: The Centenary Edition* published by Weidenfeld and Nicolson © The Dylan Thomas Trust, published with permission. Also taken from 'Fern Hill' by Dylan Thomas, from *The Poems of Dylan Thomas*, copyright 1945 by The Trustees for the copyrights of Dylan Thomas. Reprinted by permission of New Directions Publishing Corp.

All material by Karen Gershon published with permission of Stella Tripp

'Lady of Letters' in *Talking Heads* by Alan Bennett published with permission of Alan Bennett

The right of Vanessa Rosenthal to be identified as author of this Work has been asserted by her in accordance with sections 77 and 78 of the Copyright, Designs and Patents Act 1988

ISBN 978-1-913062-83-5

A CIP catalogue record for this book is available from the British Library

Typesetting: Jen Parker, Fuzzy Flamingo
www.fuzzyflamingo.co.uk

Printed in the UK by TJ Books, Padstow, Cornwall

Cover design: Clare Connie Shepherd

Cover image: Vanessa Rosenthal as Fanny Margolies in Arthur Miller's *The American Clock* (Newcastle Opera House, 1988)

To Judith, Nerissa, Emilia and Nigel

Contents

Chapter 1

BELONGING?

I am six years old and standing in line with my class at *cheder* (Hebrew school) and at long last I have inherited the brown, velvet dress that my sister Judith has outgrown. I've begged and pleaded to be allowed to wear it today, against some dissent from my mother. For two years I've coveted its short, puffed sleeves and its crocheted lace collar, but I've had a growth spurt over the autumn and the hem of the dress now barely skims the top of my thighs, which are mottled with pink and mauve splodges because of the cold. We are in the inadequately heated, prefabricated warehouse that stands in for a Reform synagogue on Cheetham Hill Road in Manchester. Plans for the building of a new synagogue in the city centre have been put on hold 'because of the war'.

'Because of the war' is a commonplace in the vocabulary of my school playground. Because of the war that ended five years ago there are bombed-out craters throughout the city centre. There's a bombed-out shop across the road where Judith and I will catch the bus home at the end of Hebrew classes. Willowherb grows up through its collapsed rafters. We are forbidden to play in it, but we will. Because of the war sweets are on ration; so are many other things and when we play at shop, we cut out the coloured squares from the old ration books our mother lets us have with the blunt scissors from my toy post office set.

I'm not really paying attention as we recite the '*Shema*' (central prayer of Judaism) which I've learned rote fashion. Hebrew is very inadequately taught to girls of my generation. Every Sunday, before we file off to our separate classrooms, all of us children come together with our teachers for morning prayers. Suddenly I'm aware of Miss Myers staring at me. She looks very angry, which makes her beaky, thin face really scary. As soon as the prayers finish she pulls me out of line by one of the puffed sleeves on my dress and hauls me up to the rabbi, who stands at the front. She is muttering something about the indecency of my hem line and the inappropriateness of the velvet dress. I sense that she is overanxious to ingratiate herself with the handsome rabbi. Maybe Sunday mornings provide a frisson of excitement in her bleak, spinster life. Now she's whispering to him, but not quietly enough. I can hear every word. She is saying 'Fancy sending the child to *cheder* dressed like this. It's not decent. And look at her. I don't think she's Jewish at all.'

This is 1950. My parent's mixed marriage and my mother's conversion to Judaism is still a rare phenomenon for the times. One much gossiped about behind closed doors and shunned altogether in certain quarters. I squirm on the spot. I know enough to realise there are secrets in my family; that the air sometimes parts and leaves spaces when my tall, auburn-haired mother enters a room. I know my father's family maintain only a distant and condescending connection to us. Minus extant grandparents on either side we are a family of four, in a culture that embraces family connections to the far outer reaches of cousinhood. I know I look like my mother because people have told me so and my dark-haired sister looks like my father.

There is a pause and then the rabbi whispers back to Miss Myers. He is saying, and meaning it kindly, that it's all right. That he knows the parents and that my mother is a convert. Both of them then look at me with some sympathy and the rabbi tells me to go back into my line.

Now it's spring time, nearly Easter and nearly Passover. I'm too young to make the slightest connection between the two or to know the Crucifixion occurred when Jesus was in Jerusalem to observe the Passover Festival in a *seder* for ever after known to the world as 'The Last Supper'.

Instead we have matzos and chocolate, but not at the same time. Any of the latter has to be reserved until the festival is over. For its week long duration we eat only matzos with no buns, biscuits or foodstuffs of any kind that contain leaven, to commemorate the haste with which we left Egypt when Pharaoh let us go.

On the first night of Passover we celebrate with a family *seder* at my Auntie Bessie's and my Uncle Adolph's house. Bessie, full name Rebecca, is my father's first cousin and his elder by twenty years. She is the only cousin of that generation to be born in Bialystok, then in Russia, now in Poland. Her parents, Samuel and Leah, left her as a six-month-old baby with Leah's widowed mother when they migrated to Britain around 1884. Once they were established in Manchester in a small drapery business, Leah's mother was to come over, bringing the baby with her; a task she duly accomplished with every intention of remaining. But after a year, her misery at the sight of the blackened cityscape of nineteenth-century Manchester drove her back home. She left behind her, as well as the baby, her younger daughter, Jane. Now the tale takes on a familiar Jewish twist. In due course, Samuel invited his brother Eleazer to join him from Russia and, lo and behold, Eleazer met Jane and there was a *shidduch* (match)! When Jane and Eleazer married, at the Great Synagogue in Manchester, family ties were then doubly cemented. Bessie's children and my father's children, Judith and myself, thus share the same four great-grandparents. This should make us doubly connected: it doesn't.

By the time of this *seder* in 1950 none of these great-grandparents or grandparents were alive. Grandmother Jane was alive at the time of my parents' wedding and shunned the whole event as a sign of the tragedy she felt had befallen her son, my father Leonard, in marrying 'out'. This sense of being not acceptable is one I have already absorbed in a process of osmosis: if my mother isn't, and wasn't, acceptable then maybe I'm not either. I don't know anything yet about words like identity crisis, but I will recognise the concept intellectually as I grow up and trail it behind me as I go on in life.

So here we are. Uncle Adolph at the top of the table. Bessie at the bottom with her two sons, Leslie and Harry, together with their wives and their two children apiece, arranged along the sides of the table. Our family is down the bottom, near Bessie, a woman of character and intelligence and one of the few people here who genuinely and warmly accepts my mother. We like Bessie, although her appearance startles us a little. Now in her mid-sixties, her hair is dyed jet black and pulled tight to sit in a bun on the top of her head. Her complexion is parchment white from the layers of powder that sit on her cheeks and her mouth is permanently turned down. Judith and I think it is because of the misery she must endure married to Uncle Adolph, a narrow-minded, bigoted man with eyes only for his progeny and their children.

Leslie and Harry are nearer my father in age, although it is Bessie who is my father's first cousin. The twenty years between Bessie and my father sets all the generations in a jumble. Leslie, like

4

my father, is a GP and is married to the glacial Florence, who is a rabbi's daughter, and Harry is married to the blonde, Irene.

We begin. I love the sound of the men racing each other as they *daven* (pray in an energetic, emphatic manner) their way through the Passover story, my father amongst them. Here he is a real *mensch*. But if, at Passover, we retell the story of the exodus of the Children of Israel from their enslavement in Egypt into the Promised Land of Israel, Adolph has long ago decided that the promise doesn't hold good for Judith and me, for his concentration is directed exclusively towards his four grandchildren. This is a pity because, for once, Miss Myers can't be faulted on how well she has prepared me to understand the meaning of the *seder* – a word that translated literally means 'the order'. I am thrilled by the story. I understand the symbolic foods we eat to remind us of our servitude and then of our deliverance. I enjoy splashing my finger in the Passover wine one drop at a time to remind us of the ten plagues God visited upon Pharaoh to convince him to let us go. I like the *charoset* made out of walnuts, cinnamon and minced apple that we eat on a piece of matzo to symbolise the cement we used to make bricks for Pharaoh's palaces. Especially I love the hardboiled egg in salt water we eat to remind us of the tears we have shed and of the promise of renewal that is to come. But it's a long evening before we can start on the chicken soup, the roast chicken and the dried fruit salad with macaroons. Near the end of it all, we six children have to find the *afikomen*, the piece of matzo hidden behind Uncle Adolph's cushions. We will be rewarded with a bar of chocolate that is kosher for Passover; or at least Adolph's grandchildren will be rewarded and wrapped in kisses and hugs until Auntie Bessie pulls a long face and says our names out loud. 'Adolph! Judith and Vanessa!' Every year he pretends to forget us, although Bessie always buys six bars. We don't like Adolph.

The second night of Passover is entirely different. Here we are greeted with affection and enthusiasm and Auntie Fanny makes a big fuss of us, but this family, the Sheldons, aren't our family. We wish they were. Simon and Fanny are the parents of four beautiful daughters, and a younger son. Three of the married daughters aren't present, but the youngest daughter and her fiancé, together with the brother, are here. And it's here that my mother has the status almost of a quasi-daughter-in-law. The Sheldons think the world of my father and love my mother, who came into their lives before my father. She taught elocution to each of the Sheldon daughters in turn, coming into the house on a weekly basis for several years and, when her marriage to my father was imminent, Fanny took my mother into her heart and into her kitchen. It was from Fanny that my mother learned how to cook *gefilte* fish, chopped and fried fish, and Passover sponge cakes; but more importantly it was from Fanny that my mother was schooled in the running of a kosher household. On the morning of the wedding it was from Simon and Fanny's house that my mother set out for the *chuppah* in the Reform synagogue.

Within Judaism there is division between the Orthodox movement and the Reform movement which sprang up in eighteenth-century Germany as an attempt to adapt to modern life in terms of social, political and cultural changes. Some aspects of worship and ritual were abandoned by the Reform movement leading to deep-seated division to this day between the Reform and Orthodox movements and further alienation for my father from the rest of his family.

On the distaff side there are no grandparents in our lives either. There's Auntie Polly and Uncle Fred, Aunt Ada and Uncle Jim, Aunt Edith and Uncle Ted. Really these are my mother's aunts and uncles, good Lancashire stock, from farming backgrounds all, who live in places like Bury and Rawtenstall and Rochdale. For king, country and the Church of England, which they have proudly served for generations as church wardens and vergers. Conservative, aspirational and upright people who claim John Bright as a distant relation. Great-great-grandfather James Whittam was a noted cattle auctioneer and farmer and Grandfather Farrington allegedly ran round Rochdale with a shotgun when my parents' marriage was announced, threatening to shoot my father. Visits here are infrequent and pleasant but have the tang of 'duty calls' about them. A conscious decision to effect some distance has been made by my parents to enable my sister and me to live in a single Jewish culture. Sometimes, at Christmas, we take flowers to my grandparents' graves in Worsthorne, near Burnley, and I worry and worry about all the crosses on the headstones and whether I'll be in trouble with the rabbi and Miss Myers if they find out. Guilt has already entered the equation and comes dragging shame behind it.

In short I'm already confused and must learn to live with it. I like very much the Jewish culture I'm brought up in. It's the only one I know, so I wish I could give myself permission to say I wholly belong to it. But I catch the nuances when my mother says, 'Jewish people in England don't go in for farming', or 'Jewish people go on holiday to this kosher hotel in Bournemouth.' It's confusing. Why does she never say: 'we like'; 'we do'; 'we go'. Later when Miss Myers is supplanted by a better teacher and my Hebrew has improved enough to follow the *siddur* (prayer book) at Shabbat, I hate it that my mother cannot. I like best to stand with my father who rarely attends because of Saturday morning surgery but when he does, rolls out his Orthodox Ashkenazi pronunciation with easy familiarity. I shelter in his authenticity.

On the other hand my mother's stories of rural Lancashire are inextricably connected to its cotton mills and traditions of community and match me seamlessly with other children at school. I know their culture too with its seasonal traditions of harvest festivals and Wakes Weeks, of Shrove Tuesday and May queens, of church fetes and horticultural shows as told to me in vivid anecdote and reminiscence. All very English and reassuring and part of the secret heritage I don't think I should admit to.

Here then are the rules I've absorbed at six and seven years old.

1. I am Jewish. My father is Jewish, but my mother became Jewish. Before then she was a member of the Church of England and part of its community. I mustn't talk about this much.
2. My father's family don't really approve of my mother, which makes me sad because she's an only child with no close family of her own. Both her parents are dead and I know she's very alone, without ever being told so. Also she's beautiful and kind and loves animals and poetry. At night she reads us *Hiawatha* and Robert Louis Stevenson, and Christina Rossetti and Edward Lear. In fact over the next few years we add *Oliver Twist, David Copperfield, Tanglewood Tales, Aesop's Fables* and *Christopher Robin* to our alternative and very English cultural heritage.

Now I am sixteen and I have a boyfriend. In fact I have had him for eighteen months, ever since my bat mitzvah. He must have been there in the synagogue community all the years of my growing up, but I never noticed him or had any interest in boys. They were never a feature on the landscape of my all girls' school. Instead I went through a stage of schoolgirl crushes, fixing on one of the Jewish prefects who took Hebrew Prayers each morning. In my school there were over seventy Jewish girls and we had our separate prayers each day before going into the assembly in the main school hall for general notices. Boys were simply the other gender from girls. But now what has happened to me? I think about them a lot of the time. At youth club discos, rambles in the Peak District or at the Ice Palace we are thrown together. We are gauche, awkward and tongue-tied with one another. The hormones may have been rising, but they have left us completely incapable of reacting to one another naturally.

His name is Paul and he goes to the companion school to mine: the prestigious Manchester Grammar School. This means with a gaggle of other girls we can meet at the boundary wall between the two schools at lunchtime and giggle and shriek at the line of boys in front of us, who hurl back derogatory comments and silly jokes as their contribution to the courting ritual. I've claimed him though and he's claimed me and it's enough that people know he's my boyfriend and I'm his girlfriend. Our conversation on the few occasions we're on our own consists of little beyond a recitation of what we've been up to, what books we've read, what plans we have for holidays, excursions. We don't explore feelings or discuss our hopes and aspirations. We have chaste kisses and hold hands. We are innocents.

By my sixteenth birthday we have eighteen months behind us and his two years advantage on me have seen him leave school and decide to train for the rabbinate. How? Why? When did this happen? He never told me anything about his ambitions in this direction or claimed to be religious, but then as I've said, we have never discussed our inner most thoughts and feelings with each other, although I think the whole world knows by now I want to be an actor. I suspect his decision about his future is something discussed and directed by his family. His stern Viennese father is an authoritarian who has already passed judgement on me, apparently, for wearing 'Sweet Tangerine' lipstick. His gentle mother, Kirstin, seems permanently wounded by their escape from Nazi Europe.

It's Christmas and Hanukkah and Paul is home after his first term at Jews College. The real surprise is that he's chosen to study for ordination as an Orthodox rabbi and not at Leo Baeck College for ordination as a rabbi in the Reform Judaism tradition in which we have both been brought up. We're going to an old boys' school dance just after Christmas. His vacation only started on 28 December, Christmas being just another week in the winter calendar at Jews College. We are walking up the long lane from the bus stop to the school entrance, past the iron railings that mark off its grounds. It's frosty and the sky is inky with the threat of snow. Paul stops awkwardly and turns to me. 'Someone has just told me your mother isn't Jewish,' he says. I'm so shocked by his words I just stare at him. First comes the familiar knee jerk reaction of shame, and then a sudden dawning that the shame is shared by others. They are ashamed of me. They have distinguished me from others which means I must have been talked about behind closed doors and never knew it.

Eventually I find my tongue enough to say, 'But she is. She converted when my parents got married. She went before the Liberal Beth Din (rabbinical Court). 'You don't understand', he says. 'As an Orthodox rabbi I could never marry the daughter of a convert.' The whole thing is absurd, ludicrous. We neither of us know the first thing about love, commitment, let alone whether he is correct according to *halachic* rule (Jewish rabbinical law), though I do suspect that even there he is wrong; however some damage is done to me that I've yet to realise will puncture my life and my sense of myself. I do know that I am rejected, comprehensively and completely.

We didn't make it to the dance. I forget why. Nothing outwardly dramatic happened. No tears, strong words. We both shrugged our shoulders and trailed back to the bus stop to catch buses going in opposite directions, he into Manchester and out to Rochdale and me towards Withington and South Manchester and we never saw each other alone again. Distantly I'd see him across a crowded synagogue around the High Holy Days for a few years.

Effectively I left the synagogue community after that, honing further the sense of crisis about my identity which had already begun much earlier. My mother's commitment there continued without falter. She was above criticism in her observance. So, it was from her involvement with various communal initiatives which brought her into contact with Paul's mother that I learned, years later, that he had left Jews College before ordination, had some sort of crisis and became a social worker.

Twenty years later, married with children and in another city I met a Jewish man on an arts committee I served on, who had also grown up in Manchester. In trying to place me against our shared background, he ran through various people I might have known before it suddenly came to him: 'Oh! You're the girl who was going to marry a rabbi.' The story must have gained embroidery in the interim, but I was unaware until then of the ripples it had left behind it. I had been an active participant in the youth community of the synagogue, a joiner-in of all that was on offer from amateur dramatics to debates, to Purim fancy dress parades and Hanukkah parties. Elderly women in the congregation had gazed on fondly as boy met girl and probably looked forward to an eventual outcome under the marriage *chuppah* (wedding canopy). I had not been forgotten, but for the wrong reasons; reasons that had started me on a long quest to authenticate who or what I really was.

By conventional routes my mother and father should never have met: their worlds were very different. My father, Leonard, was the second-born, British son of Eleazer, who had arrived from Russia in 1887 to help his brother run the small drapery business in Manchester. Less than ten years later, the business had done well enough for the brothers to open another branch in Wrexham, North Wales, and give themselves the somewhat grand sounding title of 'The North Manchester Linen Company'. Eleazer took his wife Jane and his family there to run the business and so it was in Wrexham that my father was born in 1904 in a solid red-brick terrace house on Rhosddu Road. The Orthodox Jewish community in the town was tiny but Eleazer was quickly respected and by the time Leonard arrived, he was president of its small synagogue of sixty-four members. Jane helped out in the business from to time to time, though she struggled with English and was more comfortable running her strictly kosher home. There were frequent comings and goings between the two brothers concerning their joint business ventures and as soon as Samuel's eldest son, Jacob, could drive he was often the messenger between Manchester and Wrexham.

Jacob was my father's senior by eighteen years and on his frequent trips to North Wales he developed a liking for the area, perhaps because it offered him a very different lifestyle from the close-knit Jewish community of North Manchester. Later, when he qualified as a solicitor, he chose to live in Wales, teaching himself Welsh and setting himself up to be known in the valleys as the Jewish Welsh solicitor. Always an eccentric, and very much his own man who never married, Jacob embodied a well-developed gene in the Rosenthal psyche; they all enjoyed being both of the community and apart from it; a trait already in progress in my father and then in me. The family finally left Wrexham when my father gained a scholarship to

Manchester Grammar School in 1915. A second scholarship from there took him to Medical School at Manchester University in 1921. By qualifying as a doctor he would achieve the ultimate emigrant dream of his father, who cashed a life insurance policy to fund his final years through to graduation. 'My son, the Doctor'.

By the time my father met my mother, Eleazer had died. Leonard was living at home in Cheetham Hill and looking out for his widowed mother and younger sister, Florence. For several years he'd been trying to buy his own medical practice, running up against the subtle but widespread anti-Semitism of the 1930s which saw him lose out over and over again to English competition. An elder brother, Harry, had already gone his own individual Rosenthal way to live in Bristol, where he practised as an optician and Florence brought in little money through her apprenticeship in a city hairdressing salon, though it was there that she had met and become friendly with my mother, Hilda.

My mother had come to Manchester from her semi-rural background to complete her training at the Northern College of Music as an elocution teacher, appearing from time to time in small parts at the Rusholme Repertory Theatre. When Florence first started taking Hilda home to Cheetham Hill, she was warmly welcomed as Florence's Gentile friend, until my father began to take an interest in her. From then on it was painful and open hostility from my grandmother and aunt. For over a year Leonard and Hilda agreed not to see each other, but the love match this undoubtedly was prevailed and eventually they were married in 1938 after my mother's conversion, against a background of intense hostility from both sides.

The love was certainly with them, but each was foreign and exotic to the other and the adjustments were heavier on my mother's side.

Hilda was very English; Leonard was very Ashkenazi Jewish, brought up in mainstream Orthodox Judaism, which he left to join the Reform Movement on his marriage, carrying with him a lingering nostalgia for its traditions and practices. Within Reform's more enlightened ethos my mother's conversion before the Liberal Beth Din, although still very rare in 1938, was, at least nominally, accepted, but would not have been within Orthodox Judaism. The divisions between Orthodox and Reform Judaism, then and now, remain deep and divisive. My father's Orthodox family shunned Hilda as a *shiksa* (Gentile girl or woman) and sat *shiva* (the period of mourning after a burial) on the day of their wedding, lowering all the blinds in the house as a customary sign of mourning. Minus family of her own she suffered but suppressed it. These were the nuances I had absorbed without understanding as a young child. It might have been easier if I hadn't been pulled in two directions by loving them equally.

Judith suffered similar ambiguities, but imaginatively came up with her own answer. Fired up by the fictional world of Angela Brazil, with her tales of dorms and midnight feasts, of cross-country runs and inter-house lacrosse matches, she clamoured to go to boarding school. In this she was encouraged by my father. A boarding school's very English appeal flattered his view of himself as a fully assimilated British-born Jew.

A year before, we had moved from the semi-detached house in Chorlton to the other side of the village entirely, into a large, mock Tudor house set in a large garden. Village seems a misnomer for the suburbs of a city as large as Manchester, but the names persisted. Didsbury village; Withington village; Chorlton village. The house stood well back from the main road up a sloping drive and was opposite Longford Park. At the rear, the row of three similarly detached houses backed on to fields that in turn led to the River Mersey embankment. Parallel and in the distance was the Manchester Ship Canal. At night I'd lie in bed and hear the comforting sound of barges hooting to each other in the night. Built in the early 1930s the house had a panelled hall and a substantial staircase to four-generous-sized bedrooms. In the bathroom was the first bidet I'd ever seen, put in as a matter of course by the previous owner, Mr Alhedeff, an Italian architect. It was Mr Alhedeff who had added the pagoda-like conservatory off the sitting room and a wing extension of a study with plans for a second bathroom that was never completed. Downstairs there were two substantial reception rooms plus a morning room and kitchen with butler's pantry off it.

My father's delight was the tiered garden, where he toiled to create a rose garden and planned herbaceous borders. My mother loved the house and their moving in signalled some kind of achievement for them both. Chorlton was not in any sense a Jewish suburb but with this move my father must have felt, in some part, he had arrived and having a daughter at a boarding school completed this view.

But the challenge for Judith in a school with only one other Jewish girl was unforeseen by either of them. There was an inherent conflict between her Jewish home life and her school life in a strongly Anglican boarding school on the North Wales coast. Her health broke down in a crisis of homesickness and unhappiness. At fifteen she came home from boarding school to go to a tutorial college and, as her lack of self-confidence and unhappiness grew, both parents became increasingly worried. The dining room table became a court room of inquisition and enquiry. What had gone wrong? Had someone done her an injustice? How could it be put right? Was there a magic solution that could set her back on course as the first born, the bright star with the academic mind and professional life ahead of her? In this my father's hopes for his daughters were atypical of a

Jewish father of that time and sprang from his own well-developed gene of Rosenthal individuality, of wanting to be different from the herd. Unusually he made no distinction over gender. What were we going to do and be in the world beyond the stereotype of wife and mother was his constant question.

While these intense conversations took up the foreground, I slipped off my ersatz Tudor dining room chair and into a different culture which I found waiting for me in Manchester. My rejection by Paul had frozen something I wasn't prepared to examine. I wanted out from under the synagogue's influence and into the burgeoning café society of the early sixties. At The Left Wing Coffee House and in the Cona Coffee Bar, I met alternatives, students and discontents, earnest political activists and sad Hungarian refugees from the 1956 uprising. It was heady stuff. I was on my way to being a grown-up.

In the Cona's murky basement, Mo and Celia Birtwell held court long before Celia married Ossie Clark and became David Hockney's muse and long before Hockney took Mo off to California to live with him as his companion. With my new friends I could have important conversations about important things. We talked about Existentialism and Albert Camus, about Jean-Paul Sartre and Simone de Beauvoir, about the Algerian War of Independence and the hydrogen bomb. Left to myself I spent hours in the lending section of the Central Reference Library, reading anything that interested me from R D Laing and Freud, to the whole of Ibsen and Chekhov, as if knowledge of the texts alone would secure me the place at drama school I now desperately sought. At the beginning of March all the talk in the Cona Coffee Bar was about that year's Aldermarston march in protest against the hydrogen bomb. I was already a member of the CND (Campaign for Nuclear Disarmament) and fast developing my own political opinions. The only logical thing to do was to put my name down for the coach leaving from Manchester city centre to take us to the assembly point for the march and to negotiate the tricky area of my absence from Passover.

In 1961 the weather on the march was atrocious; it rained every day and we were sodden by the time we hunkered down for the night in wet sleeping bags on some cold, village school floor. By the time we reached Trafalgar Square on the last day, I had enormous blisters on both heels, but nothing could dampen my conviction that what we were doing was hugely important for my generation and beyond. Here was an enormous mass of people, mainly young, making a peaceful protest and I was with them and of them. The experience was profoundly moving. Huddled under our umbrellas we were addressed by Canon Collins on the seriousness of our purpose and exhorted to sing out once more, which we did with great conviction, the words drifting off above Nelson's head into the March sky.

> Men and women, stand together,
> Do not heed the men of war.
> Make your minds up now or never,
> Ban the bomb for evermore.

> Do you want your homes to tumble
> Rise in smoke towards the sky?
> Will you let your cities crumble?
> Will you see your children die?

> Men and women, stand together,
> Do not heed the men of war.
> Make your minds up now or never,
> Ban the bomb for evermore.

Eventually Judith regained her confidence and purpose and, though still a little vulnerable, was able to take up her place at Manchester University to do an English honours degree. For its duration she could live at home and be carefully looked out for by my mother; perhaps more closely than was wise. All this attention on her made me feel neglected and I didn't like it. 'Look at me' was certainly some part of my reaction to events at home that winter. I'd taken to wearing a man's huge black sweater down to my knees and a fraying panama hat. I had a small toy panda that I swung about on an old lavatory chain in case I went unnoticed. The people I'd met on the Aldermarston march had woken me up to a world beyond the gates of my prestigious all-girls direct-grant school with its rules and petty conformity and I was now in a hurry to be part of the big beyond. I wanted to leave school and get on with it. The surprise was that I didn't meet the opposition I had anticipated. I think my father secretly applauded my strong will and individuality so like his own, and in any case I had a well-argued answer to his main concern: I could complete my 'A' levels in the autumn at a technical college. My mother was not so easily satisfied, wringing her hands and telling me I'd be leaving the school by the back door and would never be able to go back as an old girl. I'd no intention of ever doing so. Hadn't I voted with my feet? What I wanted was to be out there in the thick of life and doing a job like everyone else.

The trouble was I had several jobs and kept getting the sack from all of them which obviously I could not admit to at home on top of all the rest: Kellogg's Cornflakes; Granada TV Rentals; Lewis's Department Store; the art department of the large Boots on Cross Street, where I sold paints to Lowry because he eschewed the artist's supplies shops on Tib Lane and preferred the down-to-earth Salford girls I worked amongst. The first of these jobs at the

Union of Lancashire and Cheshire Institutes, an examining body for secondary school leavers, had set the pattern for the rest. This simple clerical job involved checking the marks on scripts as they came in from the examiners and making sure the overall total was the sum of its parts, but I was careless to a degree, though not I hope significantly enough to change the outcome from a pass to a failure. With my academic school behind me and my eight good 'O' levels I was arrogant and vastly scornful of the subjects under examination: Bee Keeping; Simple Commerce Stage 1; Cotton Spinning; Basketwork. If there was a lull in the arrival of scripts into the checking room, I sat with my feet up on the desk reading *Woman* and *Woman's Own* and inviting others, of whom I was nominally in charge, to do the same. The surprise was I lasted six weeks. I'd have sacked me as a liability much earlier. When I was asked to 'collect my cards' I naively asked what cards those would be? Worse, I was the cause of Karen Souter's sacking too, the chief recipient of my *Woman* and *Woman's Own*. I felt bad about that. Like me she'd walked out of her grammar school, but her home life was a mess of divorcing parents and ongoing war. Neither of us dared confess our sackings at home. Instead we pretended to go off to work each day, but secretly met up in Albert Square at 8.45 each morning before beginning our fresh assault on the Labour Exchange. The trouble was the only place open at that hour was a UCP Tripe shop that sold us cups of tea along with the most sickening smell that made us want to heave. If I had wanted the real world then it was justly giving me the shake I needed.

By the autumn it was almost a relief to crawl back into education and finish my 'A' levels in a technical college that gave me the nominal status of 'student' instead of 'schoolgirl'.

That spring I had fallen in love with Ian Price, or thought I had.

He was about as far removed from Paul as it was possible to be and his presence in my life put education and social life in balance. I'd met him at a student hop in the university union, to which I'd bagged an entry on my sister's union card. I was seventeen and looking for a salve for my rejection. Ian was twenty-three, good looking, suave and, seemingly, self-confident. He'd been kicked out of a first year general arts degree and now worked in the carpet department of Kendal Milne, where he seemed content to stay with only ever a lazy eye towards climbing the management ladder. His father had been killed in the war – yes, we were that generation – and he lived with his mother in Sale, spoilt, indulged and idolised. By this time I had a divided wardrobe with my Beatnik clothes kept separate from the clothes I wore on the social scene; or more accurately from those clothes I wore to attract conventional male attention. I haunted C&A for sweetheart necklines and full skirts held out with taffeta petticoats. I wore my auburn hair long, but never straight because it was naturally wavy. I was in a cornflower blue dress with scalloped sleeves on the night I met Ian: a misrepresentation of me if ever there was one. He looked like a cliché teenage pin-up – dark, tall, slim with a strong jaw and very light blue eyes. I was smitten on sight. What he saw in me I can't imagine since he increasingly found my ambition for my future and my strong opinions incomprehensible. I think now he wasn't sure of himself at all and fed on my teenage admiration of him. For nearly a year he tried to get me into bed and for nearly a year I resisted the storm of sexuality that took me almost to the brink. I saw what the risk of an unwanted pregnancy would do to my dreams. Morality didn't come into it, just calculated reality. It's easy now to forget what life was like in those pre-pill days. The body urged 'yes, yes'; the mind said 'too much to lose, no, no'. Ian was very persuasive, telling me again and again what his German girlfriend, met while he was doing his National Service, had said of his performance, 'Jan, Jan, you are very accomplished.' At the time I was impressed with that. He tried to tell me to forget London and the place I had now won at the Central School of Speech and Drama and be 'his for ever love' in Manchester, but I was bored with his mind long before I tired of his body. Manchester was the place I was leaving behind. I had my sights set much higher.

Chapter 2

LONDON LIGHTS

London was a shock. There were less than half a dozen Northerners at the Central School of Speech and Drama when I arrived in 1962. From being distinctive in Manchester, I was a provincial hick in London, mixing with a sizable cohort of girls who saw drama school as an alternative to a Swiss finishing school. Girls like Caroline Maudling, daughter of Reginald Maudling, Chancellor of the Exchequer. Girls who talked in confident voices of school days in the Home Counties and of their brothers at Oxford. My vowel sounds were excoriated in voice classes and I was miserable in a girls' private hostel in Maida Vale, run by a retired major, that catered largely for girls at Westfield College and University College London. They were pleasant but reserved their friendships for each other. My room-mate was doing a floristry course at Constance Spry but went home to Cheltenham each weekend to her pony. On Sundays I mooned round the Warburg Collection or the National Gallery, anywhere that was free. I had little social life but acquired a Jewish boyfriend, Peter, from University College London, whose left-wing views were passionately expressed. We had met at a CND meeting in mid-October when the world was holding its breath for thirteen days over the Cuban Missile Crisis. Peter got up to speak fluently of our peril. We could wake up annihilated the very next morning he said. Afterwards I went up to speak to him and to tell him how effective he'd been. We ended up in a greasy spoon café, talking for hours and frightening each other even more. Contradictorily, when the crisis was over and Russia had backed down, he took me to a talk in Senate House about Trotsky, whom he obviously admired. I've forgotten who was speaking but whoever it was, he was robustly and scathingly demolished by Arnold Kettle, who was later to figure in my life, though I could never have guessed it then. Peter hitchhiked up to Manchester to see me that Christmas and arrived unannounced on the doorstep, which put my mother, a meticulous housewife, in a tremendous flap, but he set my store high for a time. His extended Jewish family in Mill Hill were considered eminently suitable, but he then blotted his copybook with further discourses on Trotsky which enraged my father. Years later I came across his name as a trade union secretary in Liverpool, so the fire continued to burn within him. I think we'd both been courting our respective family's approval because we were both of us later to marry 'out'.

The compensation that icy winter of 1963 was the amount of first-class theatre I saw for free. Previews, as such, didn't exist then, but there were their equivalents in pre-first night performances when the house was 'papered' to give the actors the feel of an audience while they 'settled themselves in'. Notices went up in all the London drama schools for these shows and it was a scramble to get your name down for the limited number of 'comps' on offer. Between 1962 and 1965 I saw most of the shows at the Aldwych, including Paul Scofield in *Lear* and Glenda Jackson in *Marat/Sade*, together with everything at The Old Vic: Laurence Olivier in *Othello*, Maggie Smith in *The Recruiting Officer* and *The Country Wife* and over at Stratford East, a revival of Joan Littlewood's iconic *Oh What A Lovely War* that lifted me off my seat.

I devoured everything I could that I thought would make me a better actor, frustrated that I wasn't allowed near a text. Instead each day consisted of a voice class, Central was famous for the voice beautiful, and a movement class, plus endless improvisations to tap into our creativity. For a whole term we were sent off to study an animal in Regent's Park Zoo and return with a representation of its movements and peculiarities. I was quickly bored with this and deeply frustrated. Every week I trudged over Primrose Hill down into Regent's Park and surveyed the animals in the zoo with little interest. When the time came to 'show' our animals in a mimed representation, I was alarmed by the high seriousness which our acting tutor, Harry Lamb, brought to considering each one. Was this an African or an Indian elephant? Did it really hold its head that way? Or did that tiger really snarl in that manner? How interesting. When it was my turn to perform I brought my exotic guinea fowl to the front. Well it was really a common or garden hen that I'd lazily put forward with a lot of exaggerated head jerkings and numerous 'Puck, puck, puck…purks!' I was quite unprepared for the forensic analysis Harry Lamb brought to his critique of my 'guinea fowl' and I knew that I'd been rumbled. As he said to me afterwards, somewhat coldly, the purpose of the exercise was to instil in the actor a discipline and the keen art of acute observation.

In voice class I was more fortunate than I knew at the time, being taught by the famous Cicely Berry, who was later to be voice coach to the RSC. She taught us how to centre our voices, to speak the verse as if it came as an expression of our own unique humanity and authenticity. Likewise in movement we learned period dance with the famous Litz Pisk, a tiny, middle-aged Hungarian survivor in a long practice skirt who, when she demonstrated a pavanne or a gavotte, shone with a lightness and loveliness few of us could emulate; or sometimes it would be an *estampie* when she would call out: 'This is a peasant dance of the earth, my darlings. Down! Down into the earth with your feet. *Feel it! Feel it* beneath you.'

By this second term I was in an international hostel in Belsize Park and sharing a room with a German girl who came from Munich, where she worked in an academic bookshop. She had come to Foyles, of all places, for further experience in the book trade. It was so cold in that terrible winter of 1963 and the place so inadequately heated that we went to bed at eight o'clock, fully clothed to keep warm. When she discovered I was Jewish she went down on her knees and begged for my forgiveness. I was embarrassed. Between us both was the detailed horror that had come out so recently at the Eichmann trial. She kept telling me I must believe her when she said her father was really a decent man, from which I realised he had been a Nazi. I understood the shadow she condemned herself to live under, but I felt little pity for her. Instead I observed her minutely and judgementally with all the self-righteousness of youth. How could she think her personal anguish absolved anything of her stained country's record?

On one visit to the Aldwych I sat with some students from the Rose Bruford Drama School who invited me to a party on the following Saturday night. Bruford's was way out in Sidcup but I was determined to get there, come what may.

The terrace house and its arrangement were typical of most student accommodation I knew: two downstairs rooms with a galley kitchen extension off the back, in which was a table loaded with beer and baguettes and the inevitable block of cheddar cheese.

I knew no one but a final year student quickly introduced himself to me. His name was Maurice and he was already a legend within the school as a brilliant mime expert. Dancing with him, which I did for most of the night, was like being in a dream that Litz Pisk might have conjured up. He had a very expressive, mobile face and moved with sinuous grace. Various girls came out of the kitchen to watch us and giggle which seemed to me uncalled for. They asked me if I liked him and then giggled some more.

What was the matter with them? Of course I liked him. I liked being singled out by him and having his undivided attention. In the small hours of the morning we snogged on a wrecked sofa and arranged to meet the following week. I went home on the first tube, happy, with black feet from dancing shoeless. I had an actor boyfriend, well potentially I did, who was half French through his French father who worked for London underground. We saw a lot of each other for the next two months. We took in more theatre and caught French new wave films at the Curzon Cinema where I was especially impressed that he didn't need the subtitles. He had a confidence about him I admired and a zest for being alive that was infectious. Everything about him was quick and mercurial like his laughter, which took off on a musical scale. But over time our meetings in central London, the only solution to his base in Kent and mine in a North London hostel, felt unsatisfactory. There was nowhere we could be alone together. So when in early March he asked if I would like to go to Paris with him that Easter the excitement I felt was overwhelming. Nothing on earth was going to stop me. Paris to me was *Gigi* and *Bonjour Tristesse*. It was F Scott Fitzgerald and Simone Signoret. It was love in a garret with myself as the important heroine in my own fairy tale romance. For such a role I would willingly risk jettisoning my cumbersome virginity.

Getting there was the problem. I gave a version of the truth

at home and twisted from the lies I came up with. A Jewish
father guarded his daughter's chastity with rigid suspicion. I said
I was joining girlfriends in Paris who would be there already on
a sightseeing visit. That was partially true in that Maurice would
be there finishing a course with the famous mime artiste, Marcel
Marceau. I counted the days until my departure and filled my head
with imagining the rest. Once the ferry and train were booked, I
had time to consider the detail of what I should wear for this most
important event in my life. Words like robe, peignoir and negligee
floated about in my mind.

But standing in the middle of Market Street, Manchester, with
the little money I could spare from my student grant, I was quickly
defeated. C&A had nothing; Marks & Spencer was middle aged;
Marshall & Snelgrove was way beyond my budget and the tatty
shops around All Saints were alarmingly explicit. Time was pressing,
I was quickly defeated, tired and cross. Finally I made a decision and
took my purchase back to the reading room of the Central Reference
Library, where my sister was revising for her Part I finals. When I
pulled what I'd bought out of its paper bag, there was a silence while
we both looked at it; she with bemusement, me with defiance. After
a pause she said, 'I don't think Dorothy Perkins is the right kind of
place for what you have in mind.' Under the glare of the overhead
desk lamps the white cotton nightie with its half-crown-size blue
polka dots and puffed sleeves didn't signal a night of abandonment,
though I was never going to admit it. I shoved it back into its bag
and sloped off in a sulk.

In the event it didn't turn out at all as I'd planned. I was completely
lost for two hours when I arrived in Paris through ignorance of the
Parisian numbering system, where an apartment number appeared as
a fraction over the number for a single block, like 16/84. Maurice and

his cousin Jacques had missed me at the station. I'd been wandering for two hours, up and down the same narrow street, and was by now exhausted and slightly tearful when they found me. Maurice had been staying with his first cousin and sharing his put-up bed in the kitchen, which folded up against the wall when not in use. His war-widowed mother had the divan in the living room. Now Jacques and Maurice would be sleeping elsewhere so I would share the divan with Madame, a sombre matron in grey wool. I was completely out of my depth. The Dorothy Perkins nightie stayed in my rucksack but the thought of it must have lingered in my unconscious mind because I kept flinging my arms all over Madame in the night and she kept returning them to my side with the same weary refrain, '*Non, non ma petite.*' I was hugely embarrassed.

Things improved the next day with a visit with Maurice and Jacques to the Opéra bouffe to see a glorious production of *Pagliacci* but after it Maurice announced we were hitching to Spain the next day. Why? Because we could. What about Paris? Anyone could see Paris any time, he said. We needed to get away from the city and see the real France. For one more night, he was returning me to Madame's divan and would call for me early in the morning. I had no choice except to comply.

The following day we took the Métro to the outskirts of Paris and stopped for a coffee before starting to hitchhike. Maurice said we could pool our money. Pooling our money meant all of mine disappeared into Maurice's purse: the first man I had ever seen with one. Our Iberian trek took three days. Three days in the cabs of smelly lorries with Maurice chattering away and me staring out of the windows at the passing countryside. Still it was France! We smoked Galoises and bought fresh baguettes and cheese for picnic lunches *en plein air*. Springtime, green and fresh with the sap rising, even some warm sunshine. If the nights in youth hostels with separate girls' and boys' dorms were not what I expected, there was always Spain to look forward to.

We crossed the border near Portbou on Good Friday and went down into the village. Here was the Mediterranean, impossibly blue with little boats scuttling around, warm sunshine, whitewashed houses, heaven. Wherever the people were, they weren't much in evidence in the higher part of the village. We squabbled over money, ate some crêpes in a café, drank some cheap plonk and finally, as it was getting dusk, booked into a little *pension*. At last we had our chance to be alone. We were suddenly shy. Maurice took himself off for a walk, and I had a shower and finally brought out the crumpled Dorothy Perkins nightie from the bottom of my rucksack. The mirror by the door reflected back a silly girl who might have been just about ready to lean out of a window in any episode of *The Little House on the Prairie* but I ignored her, smothered on my *Je Reviens* and lay down on the bed and waited for Maurice.

And waited and waited. It got dark and cool outside and cool inside. Too cool not to get under the covers, at least for a short while. Where was Maurice? Had something happened to him? Should I be worried? Not that much because I fell asleep and the next thing I knew it was morning and the sun was hitting the slatted blinds in the window and Maurice was sitting in the chair beside it, fully dressed, watching me.

Neither of us had the vocabulary to deal with the situation. Was I not attractive to him? Clearly and fundamentally I wasn't. I felt ashamed and stupid. Ridiculous in my silly nightie and humiliated. He must have felt something of the same but without the courage to explain himself. All the intimacy of our London trysts from those winter months had disappeared completely. He did tell me, when I asked him, that he'd walked for a long time and then come back in the early hours and slept in the chair. Now he announced we were setting off back to Paris that morning.

Apparently just crossing the border was the goal or the dare, though none of this had been made clear to me at the outset. We toiled up the hill to the main road in moody silence and had a long wait for any kind of car or lorry because it was Easter Saturday. By nine o'clock in the evening we'd been travelling nearly eleven hours and reached a small village north of Lyons. At a crossroads in the vastness of rural France on Easter Saturday, we got out of a car in the gathering dark and as its tail lights disappeared into the distance, I patted myself down and suddenly wailed out, 'Oh no! I've left the small rucksack on the back seat of that car. It's the one that has our passports in it.' Maurice swore at me in French and kicked some stones about, not trusting himself to say more while I just stared at him. My silence enraged him more and he began ranting about the seriousness of the situation I'd landed us in through my absolute stupidity. Where on earth were we going to sleep that night? Did I know? Had I thought about that? We'd very little money. Now nearly ten o'clock, it was getting colder; we were shivering without jackets. Eventually enough common sense returned to replace the panic. I suggested we should walk down into the village in search of the local gendarmerie. After more haranguing we set off in silence.

Everything was silent and shuttered for the night, with just the occasional dog barking as we walked on. Midway down the street a blue light above a nondescript single storey building identified the gendarmerie. It was such a relief I felt like crying, but the chubby gendarme who opened the door was irritated at being disturbed. Maurice leaned against the wall outside in despair or disgust and left me and my inadequate French to explain our predicament. I tried to do just that with the aid of gestures where necessary, a raised thumb for hitchhike, 'brum, brum' for a car, followed by '*passeport*' and 'est disparu' repeated many times. The gendarme seemed disinterested; already he had taken a dislike to me, plucking at my black sweater and asking me if I was a 'beaty-nikky' and did my father know I was gadding around France in the middle of the night? Of course he didn't and suddenly I felt overwhelmed. Maurice had washed his hands of me and remained outside; in fact his withdrawal from the whole thing led entirely to what followed. The gendarme picked up the telephone and spoke rapidly to someone for a few minutes and then pushed me through the door to join Maurice. He indicated we were both to follow him down the steep, unlit street.

Towards the bottom we were keeping parallel with a high wall that ended in a large gate. Beside it was a long rope, which the gendarme pulled vigorously. A bell clanged mournfully out into the night above our heads and after a moment a nun's face appeared in a small window beside the gate. Streams of voluble French passed at a rate of knots and then, after an interval, we heard footsteps on a stone floor and the sound of keys, many keys. The gate creaked open and we were ushered inside by the same nun we'd seen at the window. The gendarme tipped his cap at her and disappeared into the night.

By gesture the nun, in full traditional habit, led us down a long, stone-flagged corridor that had pointed doorways set into it. At the last of these, she took a long key from the large collection at her belt, opened the door and gestured us to go inside the room beyond. And then without further ceremony, murmuring 'Bon nuit', pulled the door shut and locked it.

We were in pitch dark. Only as our eyes became accustomed to the gloom could we make out the dimensions of a stone cell. Against each wall was a narrow pallet covered with a thin blanket and beside it a wooden cabinet. In whispers our squabbling continued. 'Look where we are,' Maurice said. 'Do you realise we're in some kind of nunnery?' 'I do know that,' I said, 'and I've said I'm sorry but right now I want the loo.' 'Well you can't,' Maurice told me, 'You'll have to wait.' 'I can't wait,' I said, 'I'm bursting.' He scrabbled around in the dark and fished out an aluminium chamber pot from under one of the pallets. 'Well use that,' he said nastily. I was horrified. How had it come to this? I didn't deign to answer him but collapsed in exhaustion on to the thin mattress nearest me. He must have done the same because after a time I heard his regular, deep breathing and, thinking he was asleep, I cautiously got up and felt for the chamber pot. The noise of me relieving myself against its metal base sounded like Niagara Falls. Maurice woke with a start and called out, 'What are you doing?' I thought that was obvious and told him to shut-up. After what seemed a long time I heard him get up and perform the same function.

Somehow we must have slept and it was morning and bells were pealing out on every side for an Easter Sunday in the Catholic church. Sun was coming through the crack in the blinds. The same nun unlocked the door and came in with a tin tray containing two chipped bowls of hot chocolate and two hunks of bread and said brightly to me: '*Alors, ma petite, est ce que vous avez bien dormez?*' I answered politely, 'Yes, thank you.' Then she turned to look at Maurice, still motionless under the blanket. '*Et votre frère?*' she asked. After everything else this was too much. 'That's not my brother', I shouted, 'he's my boyfriend. Well he was *meant* to be.' The tin tray shook as she banged it down on the cabinet and fled with many 'Ohs' and 'Ahs!' I don't know how many Hail Marys she must have needed to expiate the sin of locking us in together to enjoy our carnal relations in a nunnery.

We were rescued by the same taciturn gendarme from the night before who turned up at nine o'clock that morning. Mercifully, the car I'd left the rucksack in belonged to a local man who lived in the next village. In daylight he had found the rucksack, opened it up to check for a name and discovered the passports. His calculation, that we were probably not far from where he had us dropped us, was confirmed when he'd telephoned the local police station. Now he was on his way to return the rucksack with the precious passports. We had been incredibly lucky.

On the ferry back to Dover we weren't speaking at all, except once when Maurice said waspishly, 'You should throw away that orange cake make-up. You don't know how to put it on and you end up looking like some kind of sick giraffe.'

Poor Maurice. It was brave of him to try to will himself into what he wasn't in order to conform and poor, silly me who hadn't the wit to realise why the girls in the kitchen at the party giggled at the sight of Maurice dancing with a girl. He had no vocabulary to tell me he was gay and I hadn't the wisdom and experience to make it easier for him.

Ten years later I bumped into him with his boyfriend in the circle bar at the Leeds Opera House on the opening night of *The Magic Flute*. The programme had him credited as choreographer for the mime sequences in the opera. By this time he was established very successfully as mime arranger to several opera companies in England, Scotland and Australia. For several minutes we made stilted conversation, both of us pleased to see each other but inhibited from bringing up our past connection. The tale of our French misadventure was one I'd told frequently against myself to various girlfriends over the years but it wasn't a subject to bring up in front of his boyfriend.

In 2003 some chance remark when I was babysitting my

grandsons at my daughter's house brought it up again and I mentioned how successful he had become. 'Let's look him up,' she said. All the laughter in the room leaked out when I read the entry on the web. Maurice had died of AIDS in the late 1980s. How could that have been and I had not known? While I'd been busy in my career and bringing up children he had already gone at only forty-five and taken with him all that litheness and beauty. Rest in peace, Maurice.

That year, 1963, I went to see the rabbi, the same rabbi who had kindly explained my parentage to Miss Myers. After nearly a year of swimming in the pool of student life, up against people of very different backgrounds and landscapes from my own, I was again in confusion about my identity. If I didn't know who I was from the inside, maybe someone could tell me from the outside. I told him I didn't know where I belonged and I wasn't happy about it. He pointed out that any unhappiness I felt was my parents' fault. The 'sin' was theirs in marrying outside of their expected backgrounds. They were to blame, not me. Oh dear. This floored me. Now blame had joined shame in the mishmash of my muddle. Was I thinking too deeply about it all, he suggested? After all this was my community. This was where I'd grown up, had my bat mitzvah. All I needed was to be put in touch with some nice Jewish boys in London and everything would be OK.

That autumn they appeared on my horizon, summoned to sort me out. Both Oxbridge graduates, from welcoming North London families. Both about to enter Leo Baeck College to train as Reform rabbis, and destined to make large contributions to the community as a whole over long careers. For a while I was invited to Friday night *shabbos* dinners and introduced to young people's cultural groups, based out of the St John's Wood synagogue, where I was welcomed in with heightened enthusiasm, which made me suspect my history had gone before me. I was the self-labelled hybrid who didn't, or wouldn't, quite fit in and thought about things too much. What I couldn't articulate was how much I envied them the careless certainty of their belonging that I longed to share. In my intellectual judgement on myself I wasn't the full thing. Paul's words had become an ear-worm in my head that I couldn't shake out. I perceived their kindness as patronisation and drew back.

Better to put the whole thing on hold and get on with the 'now' of my life in the bedsitter I'd moved into on Adelaide Road, Chalk Farm. Hurrah for the end of hostel living. Here was self-autonomy and adventure. My room on the fourth floor had a sloping ceiling that I papered over with theatre programmes and an odd sisal carpet that kept losing fibres. Rent was £2.50 a week which I handed over to Mr or Mrs Brown, the landlords, who lived on the ground floor with a sitting room with French windows that opened out on to the long, walled garden at the back. In return for the rent I was given two clean sheets and two pillowcases each week and expected to clean my room with the communal carpet cleaner that lived in a cupboard on the first floor, and to share the bathroom with the nine other occupants of the house. The two other small rooms on the top floor were occupied by Liza, who was a nursery nurse, and Charles, who worked in an office. Together we shared the small top floor kitchen, where we each had a shelf in a food cupboard and the use of a meat safe that stood on a side table with a butler's sink beside it. The gas cooker was ancient and heavy and belonged to a pre-war era. I ignored it and lived on apples, cheese and cigarettes. Here was the life in a garret I had dreamed of, and if it wasn't quite Hampstead, I could pretend it was to everyone outside London. I lay on the bed with its Indian bedspread and looked up at the sky through the skylight window, satisfied at what I'd achieved.

Manchester was dull and provincial by comparison. King Cotton was in rapid decline with nothing yet to replace it. All its proud civic buildings only underlined a past left-over glory. I chafed at my time spent there over the Christmas holidays. By New Year's Eve I was bored and restless, even my old haunts no longer held any attraction. I mooched about and grumbled at the interruption in my real life. When my friend, Margaret, suggested we could gatecrash a party given by friends of hers in Withington, I was less than enthusiastic. In my eyes Margaret had given in too easily. The stalwart goalkeeper of Pendleton Girls High's hockey team, she had failed her exams at Westfield College, London, and come back to Manchester to work as a laboratory technician in the university physics department. I knew what her friends would be, youngish academic couples from the maths and physics department, who drank at The College Arms, where they flattered themselves they formed an intellectual coterie that nominally, to her great delight, included Margaret. Their party would be as dry as dust with boring men and dowdy women in dirndl skirts hee-hawing over some anaemic punch. We kept arguing in the pub so long as to whether to go or not that by the time we arrived it was after midnight. Some couples had already left to get back to baby-sitters. Those that remained were mainly men so girls were in short supply, which meant we were welcomed in with hectic enthusiasm. Men surrounded us immediately. Who were we? Did we come from Manchester? I heard myself say affectedly, 'Well actually not really. I live most of the time in Hampstead. I'm a drama student in London you see.' Oh, they were impressed. One scurried off to get me a drink. Another went in a different direction to bring food. They jostled each other in the door to be the first to fetch and carry, except for one man in a brown suede jacket, who leaned up against the fireplace watching me in a way that suggested he was laughing at me. I was piqued by his lack of proper attention. So piqued I crossed the room and said, 'So who are you?' 'I'm Jim,' he said. 'And what do you do, Jim?' I asked, with the kind of nonchalance I thought appropriate. 'I answer the telephone and I open the letters at the university when I'm not selling the *Daily Worker* outside the union,' he said. 'That sounds interesting,' I said stupidly. He smiled some more, 'And I'm divorced and I've just broken off my engagement to a French girl.' He was twinkling at me but I was floored; a divorced communist in a suede jacket who was obviously not Jewish and obviously a lot older than me, thirteen years in fact. Here was everything that was so embargoed for me. Here was everything that was so right for me and for him although it took me two years to recognise it. Years in which he had the wisdom to let me grow up and experiment with the world and other boyfriends and start to be a professional actress.

For a year I think he was amused and challenged by me on our many dates when I was in Manchester. He watched me moving out into the world with an almost vicarious pleasure that he felt cheated out of by his early marriage to a fellow student when he was only twenty-one. Now thirty-three, he'd spent nearly half his life in academe, going up to the University of Leeds on a county major scholarship at seventeen and continuing in that life as an administrator, which was in itself a compromise from the journalistic career which he had wanted and looked set fair to gain. On graduating with a first-class honours degree in English, he'd been offered a job on the *Yorkshire Post* by Sir Linton Andrews and turned it down. He'd inherited the cautions of his working-class background, growing up in a North East Lancashire cotton village. Journalism, like theatre, was precarious. Where were the guarantees? The assurances of future security? Instead he'd wanted to prolong life in the ivory tower, entering university administration in Manchester at a point when it was becoming rapidly professionalised.

This enabled him to operate in the world of university politics which was his natural milieu. Political engagement began for him early on and was a central part of him all his life. As a schoolboy Young Tory he had drawn attention to himself in national debates and consequently been chosen to represent youth at the 1947 Conservative Party Conference. This meant that as the youngest delegate he was invited on to the podium and introduced to Harold Macmillan, Anthony Eden and to his hero, Churchill. Yet only a few years later he was in the Communist Party, recruited by his tutor in the English department, Arnold Kettle.

Arnold was well regarded within the party and with his encouragement Jim quickly found his place as secretary of the Leeds University Union Communist Party and was elected to the National Student Committee, which met at headquarters in King Street, London. In 1953 the Student Committee voted to form a delegation to attend the World Federation of Democratic Youth Festival in Warsaw. Early on, after their arrival, Jim was made editor of the English edition of the *Congress Daily*. He said this wasn't particularly arduous. All he had to do was check the English as the speeches came in each afternoon from the translator and provide a commentary here and there.

Fred Jarvis, President of the National Union of Students, headed the British delegation and in his speech spoke of the seventy per cent of British students who were already grant aided and that the proportion was increasing annually. Jim was keen to put this important sentence in the English edition, from which, on this occasion, self-evidently, the other language editions would be translated. But when he went to check the *Congress Daily* next morning, he saw that his sentence had been tampered with by the Russian translator, and in all the other editions, to imply that Jarvis was not speaking the truth.

This was a tale I heard many times from Jim over the years. Power, real power, had asserted itself and left him disquieted. At the end of the conference, he was offered the editorship of the *World Student News*, that would have seen him based in Warsaw for a year, and turned it down. Being behind the Iron Curtain so soon after the war and seeing what he saw made deep impressions on him and began a process of evaluation that eventually led to his resignation from the party after Hungary.

But for the next three years he remained active, ostensibly doing post-graduate research, while successfully putting off making any serious career choice. He had been invited to move into the top floor flat in Arnold Kettle's large Victorian house on Moor Road, Headingley, where he mixed with the constant stream of visitors and house guests who came and went. People like Eric Hobsbawm, Doris Lessing, Hyman Levy, E P Thompson and others. In later life he questioned why he had joined the Communist Party at all and concluded that in the end it was a lot to do with his admiration of Arnold, and his fervid wish to join that layer of society he thought of as 'middle class intellectual'. Life in the Kettle household gave him access to some brilliant minds and he was always grateful for the opportunity it had afforded him to sit at the feet of the great. Long after he had fallen out politically with Arnold and his wife Margot, he acknowledged this debt with affection and kept loosely in touch with them and with their sons, Martin and Nicky.

His last meeting with Martin was a few years after Arnold's death in 1986. Martin had come to Leeds to carry out a bequest in Arnold's will of the gift of a painting to the university art gallery, and there was a small reception. I watched as Jim and Martin talked on friendly terms with the shared past history of Martin's early childhood between them but there was little real connection or warmth. Martin was already writing for the *Guardian* and seemed remote and aloof from the occasion and from his home city. Whether or not there was a family party-line to the effect that Jim had betrayed Arnold in some way when he left the party, and then compounded it by becoming part of the university establishment, was impossible for me to judge. Jim's ex-wife, Polly, a fellow English graduate and party member, remained loyal for many years to Arnold's circle. Perhaps it was no more than the fallout of the divorce when friends found themselves choosing a side and Arnold and Margot had chosen theirs.

The party and the Kettles were part of Jim's stories that I thrived on in this early period of knowing him. My horizons were broadened by his perceptions about people and situations and he was fascinated by my background and ambition. Initially every date contrived to see us back at his bachelor flat, where his objective was to seduce me into bed but after my French misadventure, I was having none of it and said I was being treated like a sex object and didn't like it. Why did we never go anywhere? See anything? His response was an unrelenting rota of opera, theatre and concerts, before depositing me back at the parental home at the end of each evening with a peck on my cheek. In this game I couldn't win but nearly did when he teased me in a sexually explicit letter sent after my return to London that spring. I took a red pen and slashed it through in bold diagonal lines, wrote at the top 'This is not acceptable', put it in its envelope and sent it back. If we were at an impasse it was a comfortable one in which I was too much in the moment to evaluate the honesty that marked my dealings with him. For several months we weren't in touch, without any sense of an ending between us, rather a pause in our unacknowledged important connection.

I still had a path to follow with another fifteen months to do as a student and a social life amongst my contemporaries. At one time I had a boyfriend who lived in a ground floor flat in Kilburn with three other boys. Together they were known for throwing terrific parties but were fed up with the boys from the flat above, who gate-crashed the parties and tried to take over. They were in some kind of band I was told. What kind of band I wanted to know? Does it have a name? The Rolling Stones or something like that was the dismissive answer I received. On one occasion I met Keith Richards stumbling out of the bathroom, looking stoned, followed by an intense looking girlfriend with black hair and white lips. I envied her white, knee-length Courrèges boots as they passed me on the narrow landing and tried not to think of what they'd been doing behind the closed bathroom door. The sixties were taking off. At all costs I must play it cool and not reveal my provincial shock at the drug taking and the sexual freedoms I was seeing all around me.

Starting as a whisper, word floated round Central that there was a GP on Fellows Road who would prescribe the contraceptive pill to unmarried girls providing you could convince him you had a steady boyfriend. We rehearsed each other in faultless performances, treating the whole thing like one of our improvisation classes at Central. I so much believed in my fictitious man and where he lived and how we met, that it was almost a disappointment to leave the surgery with the precious script in hand but no man on my horizon. This totally pragmatic response to my defloration was another aspect of the self-autonomy I was now enjoying. I would be in charge of my biology, not the other way round. This was the demarcation line that marked us out from our mothers' generation. From it sprang the fashion and the music. New freedoms were on offer, if one had the courage to take them.

I set out to meet my fictitious man in the flesh and did so in the

Washington Arms in Belsize Park. He was called Ken and was a sweet man studying engineering at Queen Mary's College. He loved mountaineering and we had little in common but he was very gentle and looked wonderful with curly gold hair and a rugby player's body. After our first night of making love, I felt triumphant. At last I'd freed myself from my cumbersome virginity and the farce of moving to the brink and then protesting, 'No, no', like some Victorian girl with the vapours, but I knew nothing about my own sensuality or real sex come to that. This didn't stop me hiking over to Haverstock Hill to the house-share my sister was living in that year while she did her teaching diploma at London University. I hammered on the door at eight o'clock on a Sunday morning and announced triumphantly to her open window, 'Judith! I've done it! Last night.' She knew immediately what I meant and came downstairs in her dressing gown to ask me, 'What is it like?' 'Well,' I said with authority, 'it makes you very hungry.' 'Really?' she said. 'Yes', I said. So she made me some jam sandwiches which I ate on her doorstep while she watched me with wary, new respect.

That summer I went to Israel to work on a kibbutz. The cost of my passage there, on a boat sailing out of Venice, was an early twenty-first birthday present from my parents, given at my request. I needed to see if I belonged, not just to the kibbutz, not just to Israel but to it all of it, full stop. I was still painfully wrestling my place.

Machanayim was in the Upper Galilee close to the Syrian border and the Golan Heights. Within hours of disembarkation from the ship in Haifa, we were being taught how to assemble and dismantle a Sten gun on the kibbutz lawns: an immediate prerequisite of our stay. Night skirmishes, from across the border, were real and frequent with guard duty on the kibbutz perimeter taken very seriously. There had been many incidents, some of them fatal.

Machanayim had 200 kibbutzniks and was originally founded in 1898 by Russian Jews fleeing pogroms. By 1964 it had settled into a well-practised agricultural community, growing mainly peaches, oranges and apples. I still have the dog-eared diary I kept while I was there, which vividly records my first impressions.

Machanayim. 18 July 1964
My general impressions of kibbutz life are somewhat confused. The basic principle of life here is work. This necessarily breeds tough, seemingly unemotional people who accept that the whole of their married life will be spent in a sort of prefab tiled chalet and that all their other choices will be decided for them by a communal vote. So right now everyone is listening to Bob Dylan and Joan Baez, reading William Burrough's *The Naked Lunch* and looking at Chagall prints on their walls. I admire it as well as feel alienated by it all. Anyway it's very hot. We rise at 4.30, rush down to the communal shower block, then the dining room for some tea and then pile on to the tractor and up to the orchards. The tractor brings us back at 8.00 for breakfast. Afternoons, when the sun is at its hottest, are supposedly free until 4.00 p.m. The days are physically hard work but we have been told we'll be going on a trip sometime soon to Ein Gedi and the Dead Sea. One feels it's all part of a plan and that we are also being looked on as possible recruits. I alternate between really enjoying it like a sort of pioneer and feeling claustrophobic with all this subtle propaganda going on all the time.

Most of the girls I went with were a few years younger than me, still the feted schoolgirl daughters of North London Jewish families with aunts and uncles in Tel Aviv and Netanya. We'd little in common.

For most of the journey on the ship I had avoided them and sought out other young people with whom I'd explored the waterfront at Corfu and the Acropolis when we docked there at dawn. Now I was sharing a hut with six of these girls who had grown up together in Hendon. I didn't fit in and they didn't like me. They said I was bossy and full of myself and objected to me borrowing their shorts and T-shirts, although to my face they'd freely offered the loan of their clothes. Mine, such as they were, came from my student grant and weren't adequate for the heat or the need for frequent changing. I've no doubt I displayed a certain cavalier presumption in helping myself once the initial permissions had been given. Things reached a head one hot night when they had had enough of me and decided to evict me from the hut and sought the authority to do so. At first I was amused but then dismayed when I was summoned by the kibbutz leader, Moishe, to explain my side of things. He sympathised with the problems that sprang from the age differences between sixteen-year-old schoolgirls and a twenty-year-old student but now he had a problem. Where to put me? While he considered various options I sat on the stoop of the communal hall and felt sorry for myself. Self-indulgently I ran the present scenario into my general angst about identity and felt rejected once more. I needed someone in my corner and decided to write to Jim. I was surprised and pleased when he wrote back. He told me that my letter had reached him eventually in spite of being addressed to a newsagent's fifty houses away but it had a stamp on it at least, unlike some of my others. Sadly true. He told me not to make too heavy weather of my procrastinations about communal life. I wasn't emigrating there, or at least he hoped I wasn't. My problem was, he said, that I was a revolutionary conservative, or perhaps it was the other way round. More seriously he did say he could imagine a lot of the indoctrination I was getting from his time in the party. I shouldn't absorb too much of it but always remember what Groucho Marx said, 'Any club that would accept me as member, I wouldn't want to join.'

The familiarity of our exchanges was deepening. I couldn't put a label on it but more and more he occupied my thoughts. By the time he met me on my return there was no question of where we were at. The start of our *affaire* was inevitable and I flung myself into it with excitement. I was falling in love with him without a thought to the future or where things were going between us. Not yet twenty-one, I was living entirely for the moment. If he was more bothered at nearly thirty-four he didn't share it, nor the logistical problems that now faced us with my return to London for my final year starting in mid-September. As often as he could, he drove down for the weekend but the 200-mile, non-motorway drive, was not something he could do that frequently. As the year went on, I became more driven about my final shows, future employment, finding an agent and closed off from anything that distracted me from this central purpose. I loved him but began to have doubts there was any future for us. We lived in two different cities.

In January he was in London but didn't contact me for reasons I understood. He had driven down from Manchester to pay his respects at Churchill's lying in state, queuing all night to file past the body in Westminster Hall. Before that he had stopped off in Bladon and visited St Martin's Church. It was snowing, he told me, and no one was about, only himself and the gravediggers preparing Churchill's burial plot for the private family funeral the next day. I've no idea how long he stood there with bowed head but I recognised that it was an intensely private moment for him and he would not have wanted the distraction of a girlfriend on hand. From there he drove on to London to stay with a friend in the Foreign Office,

David Walker, who had a staff apartment overlooking Whitehall with a good view of the state funeral procession the following day. But that wasn't enough for Jim, who insisted David must accompany him to join the queue filing through Westminster Hall or he would never, he said, be able to look his grandchildren in the face. By this time the queue was a mile long and the average wait, in temperatures well below freezing at 2 a.m., was approximately three hours.

Nine years old at the outset of the war, it had shaped him in many ways. Excitement, danger, suspense, even fear all came out of the Bakelite valve radio to which he glued his ear every night. He followed precociously the course of the war on its Western and Eastern fronts, keeping notes in a self-made diary in which, on several pages, he had doodled Churchill's name. Passages of Churchill's speeches he could quote in full. Over a lifetime, the intensity of his feelings from that time was encapsulated in nostalgia for his boyhood when it was clear and unambiguous, without the later ambivalences he felt about his working-class background.

His visits to me in February and March were fun when we walked on Hampstead Heath and drank at Jack Straw's but in May we had a spectacularly bad weekend when he arrived fired-up about the mess he said Harold Wilson had got the country into and what did I think? I said I'd more important things to think about than Harold Wilson. Things like my final shows, working on audition speeches, finding a job. He looked at me in disbelief. Did I never read a newspaper? No, I said, I didn't, not when I was so stressed about *real* things. I said it deliberately to provoke him. I couldn't cope with him there in my small room with all my unresolved future in front of me. In those final weeks at Central I was in a general panic and his life seemed so worked out and set. He tried to calm me but I was closed in on myself. We went out to see *The Night of The Iguana* at the Savoy Theatre with Vanda Godsell and Sian Phillips, but things were strained between us. Walking back along The Strand in silence he stopped and took my hand. 'I don't think things are going to work out between us,' he said. 'Let's go back now and I'll collect my stuff and be on my way. I mustn't hold you back even if I want to. I'm old enough to know it doesn't work like that and you'd resent me for it in the end.'

I didn't let myself think. I couldn't think I was in such pain. I didn't begin to have any reaction until I received a letter from him on the Tuesday morning to tell me his father had died suddenly and unexpectedly of an aortic aneurysm at only sixty-four, less than ten hours after his return. All he felt now he said was emptiness and ache. Suddenly none of my current pressures were of any significance whatsoever. It was a white moment of clarity about him, about us and everything I might lose. All I wanted was to get on the first train as quickly as I could and reach out to him and tell him how much I cared about him.

We sat in the dark in his flat on Burton Road and he wept and told me he couldn't believe I'd come to him just like that. He told me things from the essence of himself. Things about his father, a trained mechanic, who had never completely understood his clever son, just loved him, and about how he had despised his father's simplicity for a time before finding a way back to his goodness and worth. In that moment of confession I knew I was his safe corner in the storm of his grief, and possibly his safe corner beyond that, just as I knew that he was mine and had been for some time.

We snatched a few hours' sleep and woke early with him urging me to get back to London in case I was late for my viva voce exam later that day. Only as he bundled me back on to the train did he say tentatively, 'I could wait, if you want me to?' I had no idea how that could possibly work in practical terms or how long a wait we were talking about but when I said 'Yes' I knew it was the big decision.

Chapter 3

BEGINNERS ON STAGE

My first job was a forty-week contract at the Castle Theatre in Farnham, playing fortnightly repertory theatre as a provisional Equity member. Then a closed shop, Equity required evidence of forty weeks continuous employment before awarding full membership on which all future contracts would be negotiated. Every rep was allowed only two provisional actors a year, so gaining one of these places was hugely sought after as the entry ticket to professional life. I was there as actor and assistant stage manager which meant as general dogsbody, I scoured the antique shops in town on alternate Mondays begging for the loan of an aspidistra pot or a Regency side table for our upcoming show, before hurrying back to rehearsal. I was responsible for setting up the show each night, giving the dressing room calls in pre-tannoy days, and then throwing on my costume for the show and slapping on some Leichner 5 and 9 stick make-up. The leisurely make-up lessons I'd had at Central were a luxury that had no place here. Every alternate Saturday we worked through the night to strike one set and put up the set for the following show. At midnight the other ASM actor and I took it in turns in the backstage kitchen to prepare a supper of soup and bread and cheese for all the technical staff and casuals working on the strike. On the Sunday we had to produce a hot meal with a pudding on a budget of two shillings per head, collected from everyone the previous Friday. I preferred kitchen duty to swabbing down the stage flats with size, which smelt disgusting, or sloshing them with paint that wouldn't come off my hands. I lived in digs ten minutes from the theatre in the home of Martin and Eileen and their two young children, where I had a room with an electric kettle and a small two plate electric Belling. I suppose my rent was a contribution to their mortgage. Martin was a successful graphic designer in an advertising agency in London and the atmosphere in the house was very easy come and go. Not that I saw much of it. From nine in the morning until eleven at night I was at the theatre. My morning walk cut down beside a field and when I arrived there in high summer it was covered in wild flowers. I marvelled at my happiness and my chance to refashion my identity now as something else.

The Castle Theatre, which seated 250, was built round a sixteenth-century barn and had its own ghost called 'Jolly Jack Tar'. The wardrobe mistress, Karen, said she'd seen him in wardrobe one set-up night when she was working late. By all accounts he was benign, if melancholy, and carried his own severed head under his arm. The town itself was leafy and pleasant and dominated by its twelfth-century castle complete with motte and bailey. On market day each Thursday, trestle tables appeared halfway up Castle Street selling local wares reminiscent of farmers markets today. Curd cheeses, local smoked meats, fresh game, home-made jams and breads. I counted myself as lucky to have my first job in such a pleasant town and not in Barrow-in-Furness or Wolverhampton, as it very well might have been. Nowadays young actors gawp in envy at the very idea of a yearly contract in which one appeared on stage every night to learn from one's mistakes and develop one's stagecraft. Well up to the 1980s most large cities boasted a repertory theatre alongside the major producing theatres in Bristol, Manchester, Leeds, Birmingham, Edinburgh, Glasgow and Liverpool.

I made my professional debut playing Mary, the maid, in the pre-war Gerald Savory Comedy *George and Margaret*. The play opens with Mary carrying in a large tray laden with toast, eggs, kedgeree and kidneys, a breakfast cooked by myself as ASM during the half-hour call. On the opening night, as I stood in the wings and heard the National Anthem coming to a close, I was trembling so much that all the dishes on the tray began to clatter and clang against each other uncontrollably, which convulsed the rest of the company. In the pub afterwards, my terrified entrance was the cause of endless retellings that grew more and more embellished as different actors got to their feet to do an impression of me. But I was ready to forgive them everything. Only three hours earlier they had given me a card signed by them all. 'Welcome to your new home,' it said. I was buoyed up with the certainty of knowing I was entirely in the right place, the place I had set my sights on years before.

That autumn the play list consisted of Oscar Wilde's *Lord Arthur Savile's Crime*; Agatha Christie's *The Spider's Web*; Sheridan's *The Rivals*; Thornton Wilder's *The Skin of Our Teeth* and Somerset Maugham's *Home and Beauty*.

Everything had happened very quickly with my job offer preceding my final weeks at drama school so that in all these weeks I hadn't seen Jim. He had moved back home to support his widowed mother before his annual summer holiday driving across Italy. Now he was coming to see me in my third professional role, straight off the Dover ferry. I was put out. Why couldn't he have seen me as the juvenile lead, Sybil, in the Oscar Wilde, in a floaty white dress with a blue sash instead of as Miss Peake, in *The Spider's Web*, the mannish lady gardener in gum boots, jodhpurs and a man's maroon corduroy jacket? I had the recent memory of the previous Saturday matinee to expunge in any case where my inexperience was woefully exposed.

At the end of Act I the police inspector questions Miss Peake on his suspicion that a dead body is being concealed. 'Where?' she haughtily responds before striding up to the armorial cupboard (I was doing an awful lot of striding in the part) flinging open its door and saying, 'Well, as you can see, Inspector, there's nothing here.' Only of course there is. Cue for the dead body to fall out. Cue for curtain down and end of act.

On this previous September matinee, all the boys were in the upstairs dressing room immediately above the stage, watching the Gillette Cup on television, where Yorkshire were playing Surrey. I reached my line, flung open the door to the cupboard only to find it empty. I froze on the spot. I had absolutely no idea what to do. Above my head I heard someone call out frantically, 'Simon! You're off! You're off.' The audience could also clearly hear it too and hear Simon's response. 'Fuck! Fuck! Fuck!' he was wailing as he pushed himself into his boots, lumbered down the stairs, ran behind the backstage flat, entered the back of the wardrobe, looked at me in terror and giving a kind of salute, fell forwards to pretend to be a dead body. It was such a howler that even now I find it difficult to think how any actor could have climbed out of it without inventing chunks of dialogue and altering the plot entirely. With only myself and Simon, a nineteen-year-old waiting to take up his place at drama school that autumn, there was no chance of a solution.

Whilst I wasn't to blame for that one, I was to blame for the next one, although I pleaded mitigating circumstances. Again it was another Agatha Christie, staple fare for reps in the sixties and seventies because the audiences loved them. This time it was *Murder at the Vicarage* and I was playing another maid, again called Mary.

During the strike on the previous Saturday night, I was consigned to packing a tea chest with props from the last show. It was gone midnight and I was very tired after a matinee and an evening show. I rubbed my eyes and my contact lenses flew out. These were the hard sort of lenses, each the size of a small pea. I shouted out that everyone must come and help me go through the tea chest meticulously from the bottom up. But they were all tired too and my request was met with a kind of hysterical laughter. They told me I could forget it, I'd never find them, needle in haystack sort of thing and if I thought everyone was going to stay on for another hour to look for them, I'd got another think coming. No, no, I'd just have to do without them.

All right for them but without my lenses I was blind as a bat. I had no spares and no spectacles, all part of a kind of carelessness that was very much part of me then and probably to a lesser degree still is. I managed to cope, with good luck rather than any proper judgement, at the dress rehearsal. My astigmatism, combined with my short-sight, meant that seeing anything in the darkness backstage was a real challenge. On the first night, I saw the green cue light come on for my entrance and frantically tried to make out where the door was for me to get on to the stage. Oh, hurrah! I could see a chink of light. I groped towards it, pushed hard at the stage flat in front of me and moved forward, with difficulty it must be said because the ground underneath me was uneven and the door seemed to have shrunk. Cynthia Grenville and Norman Jones, as the Revd and Mrs Clement, gawped in astonishment over their breakfast table as I appeared, bursting through the baronial fireplace. For seconds none of us spoke. I turned in shock and looked at the pieces of red and yellow stage gels I'd trampled through, carefully arranged to catch the stage lighting and suggest a live fire. My arrival was nothing short of a religious miracle. I'd trod burning coals to reach them. Would I ever live it down?

Nor was this end the end of my debacles, although I never knew how off-beam I was with my third howler until long after the event. Three months into my contract I did my first Shakespeare, playing the mad Queen Margaret in *Richard III*. Although far too young for the part, I had a decent stab at it and was approached by a good agent who had seen me in it and was impressed, which allowed me to think I'd been a success: a view I continued in until an incident a year later when I told Jim in a row that he'd made a 'hyeenous' remark. He held on to the wall laughing before correcting my mispronunciation, which I scornfully dismissed. I told him I knew I was right because I had said it on stage every night in *Richard III*. Then what on earth did I think it meant, he asked. Everyone knew that, I said dismissively, it meant evil like a hyena and I quoted Queen Margaret's lines at him:

'If thou delight to view thy "hyeenous" deeds
Behold this pattern of thy butcheries.'

He laughed even more. What I'd just quoted didn't even scan he said. The word was heinous. Pronounced 'hee-nus' and had nothing whatsoever to do with hyenas. Did no one think to correct me? Clearly no one knew better than me, or else they took my confident pronunciation as evidence of some scholarly research.

Jim always spoke his mind about the productions he saw and about my competence in any particular part. Naturally when he praised me I purred and when he criticised I pouted but I came to trust his honesty and appreciate it. He came down for weekends as frequently as he could and now they took on a new quality. Minus my bedsitter, it was a case of exploring different hotels in the Home Counties where the mores of the time meant I had to put a gold curtain ring on my wedding finger to satisfy proprieties. I found this a ludicrous hypocrisy that fooled no one and complained about it loudly. My only completely free day was every alternate Sunday and there wasn't much to do on an English Sunday in 1966. We walked round and round Virginia Water, up and down Guildford High Street and did the same thing in Rye. Portsmouth was a highlight. Jim positively swelled with pride as he took me round *The Victory*, as if he personally took some credit for its existence. He was deeply patriotic, very much a feature of North East Lancashire life; the Royal Navy and Churchill were sacred to him, which gave him, he said, some problems to wrestle with when he was in the party. All that was now nearly ten years behind him. In Windsor he was delighted to point out Christopher Wren's house to me and followed it with a walking tour of the town that took us up the hill, under the shadow of the Castle's Round Tower, and on to the beautiful Guildhall before we drove out to Runnymede where we stopped in the bitter January cold. No visit to Runnymede was complete for Jim without another pause besides Lutyens's Pillar and a moment to reflect on the inscription engraved on it, which, on this first visit for me, he read aloud for my benefit with a catch in his voice that I was to come to know well. 'In these Meads on 15th June 1215 King John at the instance of Deputies from the whole Community of the Realm granted the Great Charter.'

Jim's sense of his Englishness was palpable and real and I envied and admired it. I'd never before encountered it closely in anyone.

I had pride in my Jewish heritage but that was a traditional and cultural pride. His sense of being connected to the land and to the generations who had lived on it before him was not something I could match. Somewhere I think my mother had it and didn't talk about it. Israel would be the future land for Judaism that would provide the parallel equivalent but it was still new and in any case I wasn't going to live there. I was learning more and more about him and about the ways in which we, like my parents, were foreign to each other. These weekends gave us time to absorb and assess the differences in increasingly serious ways.

Time was speeding by. I was nearly thirty-six weeks into my contract. Over these weeks I gained confidence as an actor through my mistakes. I was bad in some parts, better in others. I enjoyed playing Lucy in Sheridan's *The Rivals* and Lottie in J B Priestley's *When We Are Married*, a play I was to appear in twice more in my subsequent career in different roles. I was poor as Esmeralda in Thornton Wilder's *The Skin of Our Teeth* with a very dodgy American accent. I learned how to time a laugh and handle my props and above all never, ever to upstage a fellow actor. At the end of my forty weeks, I was invited into the company as actor, no longer an ASM and no longer a provisional member of Equity: a significant milestone. My new status meant no more touting around the town for props and no more midnight suppers and Sunday lunches to cook on set-up weekends.

Just before Easter I ended my provisional period playing Mary Magdalene in *The Wakefield Mystery Plays*. The irony wasn't lost on me. Here was I standing on stage every night in a blue serge mini skirt and black polo neck sweater, saying those wonderfully, simple poetic lines:

'My bliss hath come
My care is gone
My lovely Lord I met alone
I be as blithe as ever I may
My heart is whole.'

Easter and Passover in an eternal connection.

I had a two-week holiday before the start of the spring and summer season in Farnham and returned to Manchester. Now Jim and I could see each other every day. Now we had to look squarely at where we were at and decide on the future. Were we, or was I, ready to make the long-term commitment?

Chapter 4

'LET ME NOT ADMIT IMPEDIMENTS'

It was never going to be easy for us. On paper we looked set to fail for all the reasons short-handed in our very first exchange: the age difference; his divorce; and most of all religion, the insurmountable obstacle in my parents' eyes.

Their reactions to my announcement that we planned to get married the following year were very different. They had known for some time that my relationship with Jim was a serious one. Did they think I might grow out of it? Certainly my mother did. On the morning of my wedding she tried to tell me she would finance me to go to Switzerland for six months as an au pair, hoping that might sever the connection. My father was quiet and inward in his reactions. Highly intelligent, he had the wisdom to confront his own path and I believe felt hypocritical in calling me to account too overtly. That he felt immeasurably sad was conveyed to me in new, long silences between us that tore at me. His main concern was protecting my mother from the failure she tortured herself with. Had all her efforts to provide the Jewish home she so determinedly set herself to achieve been insufficient? I have no idea what private conversations took place

My father's
mother,
Jane
Rosenthal,
in Heaton
Park in
Manchester.

My mother's mother,
Ellen Brierley, photographed
for her wedding in 1908.

Ellen, my grandfather,
Henry Stokes Farrington
and Hilda, my mother.

My father,
Leonard Rosenthal.

My mother,
Hilda Rosenthal.

Judith and me. Left: A Jewish wedding with Judith, the bride Sylvia Harvey
(née Sheldon) and me.   Right: In the garden at Chorlton.

Being made-up,
aged fourteen, by
fellow members
of the Queen's
Road Synagogue
amateur dramatic
group, in *Sunday
Costs Five Pesos*,
Manchester
Youth Drama
Festival,
March, 1958.

Now aged seventeen,
as Lady Caroline
Laney, with Keith
Bratt as Mr Purdie,
in Altrincham
Garrick Rep's
production
of J M Barrie's
Dear Brutus,
November, 1960.

Aged eighteen,
as Nina,
with Hilda as
Polina Shamrayev
in the Johnson Co.
staging of Chekhov's
The Seagull,
Stockport,
June, 1962.
Hilda is seated second
from the left.

Left: As Natella Bashavili (second left) in Brecht's *Caucasian Chalk Circle* at Central, 1964.

Below: As Lizzie in Sartre's *La Putain respectueuse* (The Respectful Prostitute), 1964.

Above and below: My first professional photographs for casting, 1965.

Above left: 'I do' and 'I don't'.

Right: Jim and I marry with no official photography allowed, 1967.

First house in Cheadle Hulme.

Jim on our honeymoon in Malta.

As Alice Fisher (Billy's mum, back right) in Keith Waterhouse and Willis Hall's *Billy Liar*, Century Theatre, 1968.

Above Left: My mother and Nerissa.

Right: My father with the ailing Emilia.

At Left: Emilia, post op., with Nerissa.

Below Left: Me with Emilia and Nerissa

in Greece, 1984.

Right: Nerissa, Emilia and Jim at home

in Leeds, 1992.

As Muriel Palmer
in Terence
Rattigan's
Harlequinade,
Liverpool
Playhouse, 1970.

As Mrs Purdy in
D H Lawrence's
The Daughter-in-Law,
Leeds Playhouse,
1974.

As Mrs Taylor in
Somerset
Maugham's
The Sacred Flame,
Chesterfield Civic
Theatre,
1975.

Above left: As
Mary, Princess Royal,
in Royce Ryton's
Crown Matrimonial,
Oldham Coliseum
Theatre, 1975.

Three plays at Chesterfield
Civic Theatre, 1976.
Above right: As
Amy in Peter Nichols'
Forget-Me-Not Lane.

Above: As
Lady Fidget in
Wycherley's
The Country Wife.

Left: As Agnes in
Edward Albee's
A Delicate Balance.

between them but they presented a united front of disappointment and forbearance. I pleaded with my mother to understand my Jewish identity was an essential part of me but only my marriage to a nice Jewish man would convince her of that. I couldn't give her that because deep down Paul had persuaded me I wasn't entitled to it.

There was pain in the house and I was the cause of it, in some awful repeat of history. My only support came from Judith. She and I shared many of the same ambiguities although we dealt with them differently. It made us uniquely close as siblings. Neither parent had experienced confusions over their identity when they were growing up as we had. We were the experts, not them.

Judith was always in my corner, as I hope I was in hers. She told me that throughout my year in Farnham, the subject of whom I might, in theory, marry came up frequently. My father felt pressure should be made to bear on me after I'd 'had my year in rep', to bring me back to Manchester and see me settled as a drama teacher. I might then be introduced to 'more suitable people'. In exasperation at yet another heated discussion she told them one day, 'I don't know why you're arguing. Vanessa is going to marry Jim.' And all of this ahead, almost, of me knowing it myself.

I fled from the unhappiness back to Farnham and the froth of the lightweight summer season of lots of Agatha Christie and children's theatre, which played through until mid-September. After the curtain call on the last night, Jim collected me and we were off on a holiday that softened the blow of leaving Farnham, where I'd been so happy for a year.

We drove straight to Dover for the late-night ferry en route to France, Switzerland, Italy, with Venice as our final destination; I was giddy with anticipation. Never had I watched the landscape of Northern France change into something lush and wooded. Place names flashed up as we drove on, Rheims, Troyes, Dijon, like myths from *The Three Musketeers*. Somewhere near Besançon, we picked up two French girls who were hitchhiking to Martigny and they sang 'Yellow Submarine' to us over and over again in broken English as they bounced around on the back seats of Jim's yellow Ford Cortina. It was all new and wonderful. In Switzerland we stopped for the night, after a long day's drive, in a chalet hotel that had duvets, not eiderdowns, and the next day via the Simplon Pass crossed into Italy to stop on the shores of Lake Maggiore. I bought Jim a silk tie from a wayside stall for Rosh Hashanah. We were at a New Year and a new beginning of ourselves.

Venice was the perfect choice, impossibly romantic and impossibly beautiful, being there and in love and away from all the angst awaiting me back home gave everything an edge of magic. This was time out, the perfect honeymoon that the real thing could never, and did never, surpass, set as it was in the aftermath of disappointed parental hopes. One night Jim sang to me on the Rialto Bridge, the sound was haunting, sweet, a song I'd never heard before. He sang it softly as light from the gondolas' lanterns cast pools of reflection on the water beneath us and the moon came up.

> *Ma belle si tu voulais,*
> *Ma belle si tu voulais,*
> *Nous dormirions ensemble lon la,*
> *Nous dormirions ensemble.*
>
> *Dans un grand lit, carré*
> *Dans un grand lit, carré*
> *Couvert de taies blanches, lon la*
> *Couvert de tailles blanches.*

Aux quatre coins du lit,
Aux quatre coins du lit,
Un bouquet de pervenches, lon la
Un bouquet de pervenches.

Tous les chevaux du Roi
Tous les chevaux du Roi
Pourraient y boire ensemble, lon la
Pourraient y boire ensemble.

Et nous y dormirions.
Et nous y dormirions.
Jusqu'à la fin du monde, carré
Jusqu'à la fin du monde.

And I hold the picture in my head to this day.

After the holiday and a brief few days at home, I returned to London and a series of temporary jobs. I had to be away from my mother's relentless daily pressure to call off the marriage set for the spring. I was very unhappy and marvel even now that I survived the onslaught. Jim was unhappy too. How did this augur for a steady future if I couldn't even be in the same city as him until three weeks before the date for our discreet, low-key, civil wedding? Why was I still attending auditions for my next job and responding to the RSC who'd shown some interest in me and called me in for an interview and audition? My answer was I was getting myself known and out of this we had one of our most important conversations. I asked him to promise that he would never try to curtail or prevent my acting career, and he gave me that promise and kept it in the long years of our marriage, even when he, and we, became 'the establishment' in terms of university hierarchy. I never joined the university wives or the university ladies club but found my own place and style in which to support him. In the early days I did feel overwhelmed by academics who asked me which university I'd graduated from and when I answered none, I'd been to drama school instead, dried up all conversation with me. But they were few, and fewer still as the pre-war academics died out and younger men and women who were genuinely interested in my different professional life came up.

Given all the tension flying around, it was inevitable that my actual wedding day was not one of unalloyed joy. My mother wanted to make it as discreet an affair as possible so that few people of her acquaintance would hear about it. Professional photographs were vetoed, as were flowers. I carried a posy of freesias and wore a cream wool minidress with a hemline that ended three inches above my knee. When the time came to make my pledges in front of the registrar, I looked at Jim in a kind of panic that he said, ever afterwards, signalled that I really wanted to say, 'Well you see I *do* and I *don't.*' Do because I loved him. Don't because I wanted the freedom to go on pursuing my career, as well as an end to being a disappointment to my parents.

Our first four years were spent in Manchester. I couldn't believe I was back where I had started out from, the place I'd vowed never to return to. After six months in a rented flat, we bought a modern 'box' out on the Cheshire side of the city. I have always found Cheshire flat and uninteresting and I didn't warm to the house, which lacked character. That it was undoubtedly a sensible investment as a temporary stepping stone to something more interesting, failed to bring me round. For Jim it was the first house he'd ever owned and represented much more than bricks and mortar. In all the seven years of his first marriage they'd lived in a flat, pretending they'd buy a house eventually but knowing the marriage lacked the permanence to see such a venture through. Now he was a houseowner and delighting in every fitment as if he'd put them in himself. I loved seeing his excitement but I was overwhelmed by the challenge of suburbia and determined to seek work in the many reps in the North of England. London was still seen by many as the only place for an actor to be based but gradually things were changing and would continue to do over the next two decades as more actors, who could not afford London property prices, moved out. Providing one accepted that the casting process always took place in London and accepted the train fares involved, the problems could be overcome.

My grounding at Farnham had given me a good footing and in the four years in Manchester I worked at Chester Gateway Theatre, the Contact Theatre, Manchester, Liverpool Playhouse and the unique Century Theatre as it took to the road.

The Century Theatre was made up of four thirty-foot long blue metal trailers that, when stationary, locked together to form a mobile auditorium, stage and dressing rooms with a smaller unit acting as a box office. For over twenty years it toured Northern towns providing good theatre before moving up to Keswick each summer for the tourist season. The year I was there we did *Billy Liar*, *A Day in the Life of Joe Egg*, *Uncle Vanya* and a spectacular production of *The Tempest*. Spectacular because when rain hit the metal roof of the stage the sound was deafening and you could hardly hear yourself speak on stage in the very appropriate maelstrom.

With all these jobs I commuted from home, driving fairly substantial distances after the show each night. My chief memory of the time is that all the work took place around my two pregnancies, neither of which was consciously planned, except in terms of my forgetfulness to take the pill. Deep down I was in a hurry to give us the family Jim was now so aware he lacked. I was pregnant by the time *The Tempest* was introduced into the Century Theatre's repertoire with Denis Lill as Prospero, launched in his first job after leaving New Zealand. Luckily I had only the small part of Iris, the goddess of plenty, which was ironical given the circumstances. What had started out as a fairly conventional masque costume of a pink leotard under shimmery gauze netting, had, by the time we reached Burnley, become fairly obscene. Over one weekend the baby had moved out of my pelvis to announce herself to the world in a huge bulge which made my participation in the fertility dance we performed unnecessary. Never mind that I was about to leave in a fortnight, what could they do with me in the meantime? The designer hastily made a ludicrous rock out of papier mâché and I was ordered to sit behind it and wave my arms out from the sides of it like some demented jellyfish.

The following summer in Chester I had the live baby, Nerissa, with me to show off after a Saturday matinee of *The Crucible* when Jim had called in to collect me. I was carrying her down the stairs from the bar when I met David Suchet coming up. David was in his first job after leaving LAMDA. He was playing Thomas Putnam and I was playing Rebecca Nurse. He stopped me and put out his arms, 'May I?' he asked. I handed her over and he held her so gently and said, 'Do you know, I've never in my life done anything as wonderful as this.' The picture holds for me yet: an image of the lovely man he was, which shows in every one of his impeccable performances.

At Liverpool Playhouse for a Sheridan play, *The Critic*, I was expecting my second daughter and heaving my swelling bosom into a Restoration corset each night, always in a hurry not to miss my nightly ritual of tying Michael Gambon's cravat in the green room before he went on stage as Don Ferolo Whiskerandos. Near the end of the run he looked down at the top of my bent head and said in that gravelly voice, 'You fancy me really, don't you,' and I blushed bright red.

The year seemed to be rushing on with much happening for us both. Jim had now been appointed a senior administrator. He always said, and said generously, that nothing was going right for him until he met me. He was in the wrong marriage, in a temporary home with no clear idea of what he wanted or why he should work towards it, even if he could identify it. Now he had the marriage, the house and the family and a strong sense of direction and ambition.

But by the end of the year life had darkened for us both. Our second daughter, Emilia, was born at the end of August 1970 and within a fortnight it was obvious she wasn't thriving. The health visitor said her noisy stridor breathing was caused by a floppy larynx, which she'd grow out of in time but that didn't reassure me. Any feed took over an hour in which she threw her head back in distress at some apparent physical cause and then wailed because she was hungry. There were nightmare days and nights with little sleep for any of us including a jealous, angry, toddler sister. I bypassed the health visitor and sought my doctor's opinion who, examining her in a rare period when she was calm, said there was nothing wrong with her. Instinctively I knew there was. After three weeks we were all so exhausted that my father and mother offered some help. They said they would take the baby for a night to give us a decent night's sleep. This intervention was the thoughtful gesture of any grandparents but at 7 a.m. the next morning my father rang, not as a grandfather but as a concerned GP. He said very simply, 'This baby isn't right. I'll write you a letter for the paediatric consultant and you must get her down to the clinic this morning.' The urgency in his voice was unmistakable.

By the time, four days later, Emilia was admitted for tests at the Children's Hospital, in Pendlebury, her head was bent right back as she struggled to take in any breath at all and her birth weight had dropped to under 6 lbs. An angiogram revealed she'd been born with a double aorta. The second, superfluous, one had wrapped itself around the oesophagus and trachea and was slowly strangling her. The cause of this congenital aberration was most likely my allergic reaction to aspirin, which I'd taken for flu in the first few weeks of the pregnancy, a time when the foetal blood vessel system was being laid down. Now the only answer was open thoracic surgery in a procedure unheard of until Christian Barnard had pioneered open heart surgery only some years before. They would cut away the superfluous aorta and, in theory, the situation would be reversed. No one would commit themselves to saying if this was actually possible with a major artery involved that was only a couple of centimetres wide.

On the day of surgery I was shown into the family room adjacent to the ward. The hours I spent there watching the clock and waiting for her return from theatre were the loneliest of my life. I was on my own while Jim looked after Nerissa at home and relied on my updates from the telephone call box by the main doors. After two hours I heard the wheels of the trolley outside in the corridor. There she was, alive but tiny, under a perspex incubator and naked apart from her nappy. Someone had taken a knife and sliced open her chest from sternum to spine in a great diagonal slash like opening up some carcase in a butcher's shop. The pity of it was indescribable and I was running cold with terror.

That night I slept in the parents' house to be on hand. I knew why they suggested it and sleep was a misnomer anyway. I lay down on the damp bed, fully clothed. In the next two beds were a mother and father who had changed into nightwear. They were obviously well used to hospital stays with their chronically sick child. I watched the shadows of ambulance headlights criss-crossing the ceiling. When a powerful torch played across the beds and someone in uniform started calling out a name, I knew it would be mine. The baby had lost a lot of blood, the nurse said. They were giving her a blood transfusion. I should come back to the ward and see if I wanted to have her baptised. I couldn't do that I said, 'I'm Jewish.' I was prepared to assert my religion but not to admit we were at crisis point or maybe already beyond it.

A white screen of doctors and anaesthetists surrounded the incubator in the intensive care booth when I got down to the ward. I stood outside the plastic tent between them and me, angry that not one of them would shift sufficiently to allow me even a glimpse of her but when they did, my anger became a fury. On the mattress were clumps of the dark brown hair she'd been born with, such a lot of hair. The destruction overwhelmed me utterly. I started yelling out at the top of my voice, 'What have you done to my baby? What have you done to her?' A staff nurse led me gently away to a chair and explained her veins were so tiny that the only place they could get a needle into her for the emergency blood transfusion was in her scalp. If the bleeding didn't stop, they would have to take her back to theatre. I gripped the nurse's hand and thanked her, crying the only tears I allowed myself. The next few hours were crucial. I knew that. I stumbled outside into the night where there was a small courtyard with a bench. From 3 a.m. until 5 a.m. I sat getting colder and colder but I wouldn't move. I knew if I moved I would lose connection with her and all would be over. Just as the sky was lightening a little, the same staff nurse came out and told me Emilia was holding her own and the bleeding had stopped. I went into the small chapel in the hospital grounds and prayed.

'We are not out of the woods,' a bouncing Canadian anaesthetist told me later in the morning, 'but it is looking good. It was incredible in theatre,' he said with a scientific enthusiasm he couldn't control even as my white, strained face was in front of him. 'Just incredible. As soon as the second aorta was cut away, her breathing note changed completely and her oxygen levels rose.' And off he went humming down the corridor.

I didn't breathe out myself until Jim arrived with Nerissa. I'd asked him to bring her. I wanted to hold on tight to her twenty-one-month-old aliveness and put her face up to mine and believe things could come right again. I can't remember that we ate or drank anything all day; there weren't those kinds of facilities in hospitals then. We just took it in turns to tiptoe into the ward and hold our breath. By four o'clock I was ordered home by a staff nurse who told me I could come back first thing in the morning but I'd be no use to anyone, least of all my sick baby, if I was exhausted. I did as I was told.

When I went back first thing next morning Emilia had been moved out of intensive care and I allowed myself to believe the worst was over. In the weeks that followed they nursed her night and day in a reclining baby chair inside a cot, never allowing her to lie down while her chest drain was in situ. I would sit in the darkened ward at night while other children slept around me and study the grey complexion of her face under her shaved head and physically ache to hold her close. She looked so sad and abandoned and I anguished over how I'd let her down.

Years later I learned that Emilia's case notes were being studied by probationary paediatric nurses. The surgery itself was cutting edge and the congenital abnormality rare, which made her case a good teaching model; also one which had a happy outcome. Apart from a susceptibility to bronchitis in early childhood that disappeared as her trachea straightened out, she was a healthy, happy little girl. When she was eighteen, I tracked down the consultant paediatrician who had first considered the rare diagnosis that had set the tests in train while there was still time for the surgery to be successful. He was about to retire from Addenbrooke's Hospital in Cambridge and I wanted to thank him for the life of her and to tell him she was now a fine young woman, bright, curious, kind and off to university. He wrote back to tell me he was touched that I'd taken the trouble but that the credit for her growing into a caring young woman was down to her parents. But neither the paediatrician nor the parents would have had the chance of any of it if my father had not made that early morning phone call in the first place.

Chapter 5

ALL ROADS ROAM TO LEEDS

'All roads roam to Leeds,' was the limp joke a professor of Spanish told me when he heard we were moving there in 1971. I laughed politely. Behind the joke was an acknowledgement of the distance between the two cities. Not in the actual sixty miles but, before the M62 Motorway was fully completed in 1976, the trek across the Pennines was a long and difficult one.

We were returning to Jim's alma mater where he had been appointed deputy registrar of the university. Far enough away from my home city of Manchester and yet still within the North. We'd found a house out beyond Roundhay: a 1920s art deco house with many of its original features intact and a half acre of garden, far more than we were really up to. The house was set back from the main road, with a long drive bordered by a hornbeam hedge, and had Crittall windows, some of which needed replacing at much expense. From first sight I loved it and made excited plans for its interior design that had to be put on hold while it was re-wired and central heating put in. Jim started at the University in the May and completion wasn't scheduled until the July, which meant from Monday to Friday he was in staff accommodation and I was in Manchester on my own with two children under three, one of them still fairly delicate but I've no memory of it other than as a time of looking forwards.

My first impressions of Leeds back then were not favourable. Leeds looked like a one-horse town, defeated by the collapse of the textile industry and yet to diversify, as it did a decade later, into financial services and light engineering. At my first university dinner I overheard an elderly, very patrician woman say in a loud voice, 'I really don't like Leeds at all. Awful city. But what I do like is that one can get out of it so easily into glorious North Yorkshire.' That might have been the occasion, or a later one, when the professor of dentistry's wife, who was Norwegian, lamented the passing of standards within the university in a doleful sing-song voice. 'When I came to this university,' she told me, 'all the ladies wore white gloves up to their elbows if the Princess Royal, our chancellor, was visiting. We lined up on the Parkinson steps and curtsied low as her car drew up.' I might have fled in dismay but there was no getting away from it. Leeds was a university with pretensions, modelling itself on an Oxbridge college, views in which it had been actively encouraged by its Edwardian vice-chancellor, Sir Michael Sadler.

Unlike Manchester with its sprawl of suburbs in the west towards Lancashire and in the south towards Cheshire and Derbyshire, Leeds was compact. Most of its professional classes lived in the north of the city, in Headingley or Roundhay. At the end of a day no one disappeared any great distance. They could return easily in the evenings for the dinners and receptions and extramural lectures. Informally there were private dinner parties and drinks parties, tea parties and coffee mornings for charitable causes. On the plus side this meant academics from different faculties had a real chance to know each other socially, giving the place a strong sense of community.

The minus side seemed, in the beginning, to be all mine. I was only twenty-seven and the thirteen-year age difference between me and Jim meant I was mixing with professors' wives in their late forties and upwards, who were not always welcoming to the young woman they saw enjoying the married professorial status that they had waited years to achieve. Yet again I began to doubt where I belonged.

So, again I returned to Manchester, to the synagogue I had grown up in, to see the rabbi. Time had moved on. They were temporally without a rabbi but in the interim an Israeli Reform rabbi was holding the fort. A small, quixotic man with expressive hands, he ushered me into his office where I regaled him with my now-familiar tale. At the end of it he put his head on one side and said, 'I don't think you need a rabbi. I think you need a psychiatrist.' That was a jolt too far. I had looked to lay my hurt at his feet and he was telling me, yet again, I was thinking too much. Only as I was leaving did he say, 'You know, the one person who can decide all this is yourself. You can be whatever you want to be.' It was years before I was to understand the wisdom of his comment.

As a young actor I read an American book entitled *The Psychology of the Actor*. I devoured it, not least for its explanation as to why the actor commits himself to a lifetime of painful rejections and long periods out of work. The answer, according to this book, is that every actor is a damaged personality who seeks in the impersonation of another character some repair to his or her sense of self: a kind of therapy for bruised psyches. If the repair is achieved successfully then the actor gives up the profession altogether and, newly whole, embarks on another career entirely. Those that remain in the business have absorbed 'their damage' and acquired years of technique and experience in the interim, making them into true professionals set unalterably on their careers. The thesis of the book made sense of my determination to be an actor from a very young age: I wanted to be somebody who wasn't me and yet even there I think it oversimplified. I wanted to be an actor because I was in love with the magic of make-believe and because I found I could make people laugh, and having discovered this, I used it on and off stage ever after. As a child I delighted in acting the clown and when I saw it could dilute some family row I made it my role within the family. Later I found that playing the clown deflected others from getting too close. I could protect my real feelings behind a well-honed carapace of 'the joker'. But I lived in contradiction of *The Psychology of The Actor*. I *was* still an actor and as the Israeli rabbi had shown me I hadn't 'absorbed my damage', or even yet incorporated it into who I was.

Back home I laid it all out on the kitchen table between myself and Jim who listened with kindness but didn't understand that my problem was about belonging, not about religion, and in any case Marx had cured him of all that. He had gone from being a choirboy in the village church to being an assured atheist who yet retained his special delight in the words of the King James Bible and The Book of Common Prayer, all of which had helped to form him culturally.

Although this was far from our first conversation on the subject, the question now was how should we bring up our children? In the year before our marriage we had had many such conversations but reached no satisfactory conclusions. Being Jewish was as much a part of me, as his being English was to him, but freed from any religious practice, he didn't need to do anything to go on being English for ever, whereas I felt I should be demonstrating my identity in some way, and didn't. In the end we settled on giving them a cultural heritage of both religions; one of those wishy-washy phrases that didn't mean a lot but did result in their freedom as grown women from any of my angsts about identity, also I believe in loss. You can only reject what you have had. By heritage they are proud to call themselves Jewish; in reality their knowledge of Judaism is patchy. Judaism was not the dominating culture of the home and I never passed on, in any detail, Jewish practice and observance. Some of this harked back to my lack of confidence in my entitlement to do so. Some of it was judging where the balance lay within my good mixed marriage. Passovers were spent in Manchester; Christmas rituals belonged in North East Lancashire where St Thomas's village church lay at the centre of everything.

Once the village of Barrowford had had eight or nine fully operational cotton mills, where most of Jim's family had worked for generations. Good folk. Tacklers and weavers, upright and Christian, for queen, country and the Tory party, that last the real surprise. Even by the 1970s the mills were all gone. Approaching from the east, the view down into the village was, and is, an uninterrupted one of farmland and dry stone walls with Pendle Hill in the distance. Before the motorway brought the city nearer, the village existed as a self-contained hub of industry in a rural setting. Until my sixty-four-year-old mother-in-law was widowed in 1965 she had never been to London; Manchester was metropolitan enough. Ironically my upbringing in a Northern city was the one of soot and blackened buildings; Jim's here was one of the country, of bike rides into the Trough of Bowland and holiday jobs on the local farm where he was once sent off by the farmer, Leo Begley, to walk a cow to Nelson cattle auction. We were nothing if not each other's opposites as we put down roots in a city new to me but not to him.

The children went to the local primary school and I was lucky to get work at the three-year-old Leeds Playhouse. For a city the size of Leeds it was surprising that until 1970 it had never had a repertory theatre. The audiences must have been there for it because from the start the Playhouse was well supported. In my first season there we did García Lorca's *Blood Wedding* and Shakespeare's *Measure for Measure*. In my second, we did Bertolt Brecht's *The Good Woman of Setzuan*, D H Lawrence's *The Daughter-in-Law* and Arthur Miller's *Death of a Salesman* in which I played The Woman. This was the first Miller play I had done and I would go on later in my career to play Beatrice in *A View from the Bridge* at the Cheltenham Everyman, Linda Loman in *Death of a Salesman* at Bolton Octagon Theatre and Fanny Margolies in *The American Clock* at Newcastle Playhouse. Working on Arthur Miller's plays were highlights of my career. My admiration of the breadth of his writing, of its compassion and humanity, which spring above all from his Jewish soul, became a yardstick from then on against which I measured other playwrights. The families in Arthur Miller's plays are always Jewish families for me, whatever names they may be called. They are not the movers and shakers of life but they are, ironically, Everyman and Everywoman whose endurance in the face of tragic circumstances gives them a dimension of quiet nobility.

At Leeds we were a young company under the directorship of John Harrison, who had come from Birmingham Rep and I was something of an anomaly: an actor who lived locally. I was well aware of the contrast. While all the actors would return to London at the end of the season to hassle for the next job, I would stay put. This security brought with it some harsh self-assessment. It was unlikely I would have that 'lucky break' every actor dreams of. Was I really ready to face that? If things went well I might continue to work steadily in the profession I loved. Was that enough? I'm not sure I ever answered it. Having posed myself the question I just went on doing what I did and still do.

From Leeds I went on to work at many of the Northern reps, places like Oldham Coliseum, York Theatre Royal and again the Contact Theatre in Manchester. During the year when Jim was in Bangladesh for a month at the invitation of Dacca University to advise on their university administration procedures, I was at Chesterfield Civic Theatre for a season doing an interesting play list of William Wycherley's *The Country Wife*, Peter Nichol's *Forget-Me-Not Lane*, Somerset Maugham's *The Sacred Flame* and Edward Albee's *A Delicate Balance*, driving home each night after the show.

Until now I had had the wonderful Ann as childminder, who collected the girls from school each day, brought them home, gave them tea and looked after them until Jim arrived home. Nevertheless things could and did go wrong when a director would suddenly announce at five o'clock that he wanted to carry on rehearsing into the evening if the company were agreeable? Being in digs and away from home the company were only too happy to have their evening filled while my stomach went into knots. This would often be the very evening Jim was at a dinner and the same evening when Ann could only stay until 6.30 p.m and I had promised her I would be home by then to take over. Somehow I had to solve things from a telephone call box in a snatched tea break. Nowadays Equity has fought fiercely to have working actresses' childcare needs respected and not penalised. Back then one wouldn't have dared bring up one's domestic arrangements. There would always be another actress unencumbered by children ready to leap at any job. Formally I had to present myself as childless which doubled the guilt I already felt at not being there for their bedtimes for weeks at a time.

Bangladesh and Jim's absence from home for four weeks presented special problems that I solved by offering a lovely PhD student, Helen, free digs in return for taking over from Ann each evening at 6.30 p.m. I seemed to live in a permanent state of tension in those years. Supermarket shopping had to be done in some strange town in a missed lunch hour, school shirts ironed at midnight, lines for the next show learned in a dressing room while listening out for my cue in the current show. I marvel at the human brain that I didn't walk on stage spouting Edward Albee when I had arrived there to spout William Wycherley.

Shorter trips of Jim's away from home posed fewer problems in terms of childcare arrangements. I might even have been invited and unable to make it when he went, with the professor of law, shortly after Bangladesh, on a goodwill trip to the University of Le Mans to foster a relationship between the law faculties of the two universities. In any event I wasn't there and heard only by report of the general feasting and formal French hospitality they received. Out of it Jim struck up an unusual friendship with André Pouille, the dean of the law faculty at Le Mans. Both had a long-term vision for the governance of a university and for its place in their country's scheme of things.

André was extremely tall for a Frenchman, very right-wing and a staunch Gaullist whose family wealth came from extensive vineyards around Bordeaux. Jim and he couldn't have been more different in all sorts of ways, but each appreciated something in the other and they got on. So much so that André insisted we visit them that summer on a drive back from a family holiday in South West France.

We arrived extremely hot and dusty after a drive of 280 miles to the cool of their garden and the warmth of his Finnish wife Majio's welcome. We were later told they'd met in Paris and become engaged but André had insisted they wait twelve months in order for Majio to speak fluent French. He certainly wasn't going to speak English in which she was almost bilingual. In many ways he was an impossible man but also delightful. Now he took over completely and while his daughters and ours of similar ages played together, he insisted we took showers, almost as if he was holding us at arm's-length for our unpleasant smell. The pleasing bathroom had a white tufted carpet and a tiled shower cubicle. I let Jim go first and waited. And waited and waited. After nearly half an hour I became worried. Had he had a heart attack in there after that punishing drive in the heat? I went to the door and called quietly through the keyhole 'Are you all right in there?' The muffled answer came up from floor level as, 'Yes, but I've got a bit of a problem in here.' I insisted on being let in to find a very pink, naked Jim down on the floor trying to scoop up armfuls of foam that were halfway up the walls. He had almost disappeared into it all like some plump Botticelli cherub surrounded by clouds of glory; except these clouds were the entire contents of a bottle of shower gel which he'd knocked off the shower cubicle wall. This was the late seventies and we were not yet used to such bathroom products. Jim was oblivious of the accident until he stepped out of the shower cubicle. Busy scrubbing away at himself under hot, steamy water, he had splashed on with abandon compounding the disaster as water escaped over the cubicle wall and fed the foam already down there into mountainous piles. Whatever could we do? We both set to, scooping up armfuls of suds and chucking them in the bath under the cold tap to disperse them. When we'd done the best we could, we were both red in the face and sweating and the carpet was damp with the smell of wet wool hanging in the air.

Downstairs no one mentioned our long absence. All the girls had been fed and were off somewhere when we sat down to dinner. André was at his best, or worst. When my bread crept on to my hors d'oeuvre plate his arm shot out. '*Non! Non!* In France it is not done to do so. In France the bread goes on the table, so, and we break it with the hand, so.' I did my best to comply, feeling embarrassed. Then, while Marjio cleared the plates, he went to the sideboard and solemnly took out a mini table version of a Moulinex hoover, passing it to each of us in turn to collect our breadcrumbs. Buzz. Buzz. Buzz, it went, with Jim and me trying to keep straight faces. By the time we reached the cheese, André must have realised he'd gone too far. 'Jimmy,' he said, 'what is it "not done" to do when dining in your country?' Jim might have said to correct your guests' table manners, but he limited himself to saying, 'Smoke before The Queen.' 'Ah!' said André, now once more the genial host, 'let us have some brandy.' Leaning over Jim he began to pour, saying conversationally, 'Jimmy, I have never asked you before, but whereabouts in England do you come from?' There are any number of answers Jim might have given, all equally correct. He could have said the North of England or Lancashire, or Burnley; instead some devil in him made him say, and this time precisely correctly, 'Nelson'. 'Nelson! Nelson!' André roared. 'Nelson! That is the last glass of brandy you drink in this house,' and the bottle went down on the table with a thump. The evening was a special one-off never to be forgotten; over the next twenty years there were other meetings but none as significant. It cemented a friendship of opposites based on mutual affection.

Chapter 6

'BY INDIRECTIONS FIND DIRECTIONS OUT'

Balancing work as an actor with bringing up a family could be a challenge because the hours were so different from everyone else's working life. At times I welcomed the easier jobs I was beginning to do for BBC Radio Drama out of the Manchester Studio along with small parts on television at Granada and Yorkshire Television where a contract was for days not weeks. I didn't work away from home until the girls were older and I accepted that this meant I sometimes had an hour's commute from curtain down in the theatre to my own back door. Like most actors I know I was forever wailing when a contract finished, 'Will I ever work again?' but secretly welcomed a chance to enjoy family life without the guilt trips I had when working. Between contracts, the rhythm of the weeks was the rhythm of ballet lessons and Brownies, swimming lessons and piano practice. October was school Harvest Festival and Halloween. November was Bonfire Night and then there was Hanukkah and Christmas. In one of these longer periods out of work I met up with an old school friend, now a senior social worker. She mentioned that the probation service was snowed under and looking for volunteers. If I had some time to spare I might find it interesting.

The application process to be an accredited voluntary probation officer was fairly straightforward. After filling in some forms and having my references checked, I had an interview with a probation officer that seemed to satisfy requirements and was given a shiny pass in a plastic wallet that announced I was now an accredited voluntary probation officer. It was explained to me that the volunteer fulfilled an invaluable role in the probation service. Many of their clients felt inhibited from talking to their official probation officer but found they could talk more freely to a volunteer. The volunteer was a sort of halfway house, part friend and advocate on their behalf, part monitor to check the rules were being kept. The important thing was to make a connection through visiting on a regular basis.

That was how I met Derek, who was struggling to bring up his three daughters of sixteen, fourteen and ten after the death of his wife, an event which had overwhelmed him. Into this household he'd now introduced his eighteen-year-old girlfriend, Audrey, who was the mother of his eighteen-month-old son, Darren, who was adored by everyone. A mangy Alsatian called Ranger, which crapped on the bare boards in the living room, completed this filthy household in which there was a lot of love and little else. Most nights I'd arrive for my weekly visit to find Derek about to set out for the working men's club down the road to enjoy the couple of pints he couldn't afford. He'd be whistling away as he scrubbed at his armpits in the kitchen sink and dried them off on the one tea towel; the same tea towel that elder daughter, Karen, would use later to scrupulously polish up the mug for the tea she made me and which I drank. I wasn't supposed to ask what Derek was on probation for, but he cheerfully told me it was for 'nicking stuff'. I liked Derek, he was a survivor: the original cheeky chappie with his slicked back black hair and his collection of bad jokes picked up on Leeds market where he worked occasionally 'under the counter' while claiming the dole. Already I knew things his probation officer didn't and worried where my loyalties lay. By now I was a welcome visitor with the girls who seemed flattered that someone they called 'posh' cared about them. Coming up to Christmas I took some presents round for the children and the baby, along with some mince pies and a Christmas cake. For once Derek was at home. The electricity was off because they'd no money for the meter until the following Friday and the house was bitterly cold as they all huddled around some bits of poor coal in the grate. The one thing that was drummed into me was that on no account must I ever give out money to any probation client. We sat in the dark for thirty minutes with the baby crying and then Derek had had enough. 'I'm not putting up with this,' he said. 'Karen give us that knife.' He took the chair I was sitting on over to the wall. My job, he told me, was to hold it steady while he rifled the coin-operated electricity meter. Audrey could strike the matches to put some light on the job. We were a joint team willing him to succeed as we stood there in the matchlight. When he'd triumphed (I suspected not for the first time) and the power was back on, we all clapped him as a hero. What was I doing? I should have been reporting stuff like this to Derek's probation officer but I couldn't bring myself to tell on him. Already I was on a path to subversion and should have resigned there and then as someone totally unsuitable for any kind of role as a voluntary probation officer. I didn't which led me into more trouble further down the line.

Derek's case was passed on to a different probation officer and I never heard any more about him. The new probation officer I was answerable to, now gave me a very different assignment. I was to collect the three young children of a prisoner in Wakefield gaol and take them in to see their father because their mother refused to have anything to do with him. Once again I was told it was entirely the prerogative of the client whether he chose to talk to me about his crime or not. All I was told was that he was coming up for parole shortly after serving his second life sentence. This was puzzling in view of the very young age of the children.

Anyone who has ever made a prison visit will know how intimidating the security process is for a visitor. I held the two smallest children's hands and tried to give off an air of calm as I waited to have my handbag searched and my visitor's pass scrutinised. The children seemed unperturbed and I suspected that they were old hands at this. In the large visitors' hall they ran towards a man with white hair already seated at a square table and gave him hugs and some crayon drawings they'd done for him. There was orange squash and chocolate biscuits ready on the table that he must have bought already from the snack bar by the door that was manned by volunteers. I stood back, feeling awkward and felt the stares of a number of men. There was a tamped-down atmosphere of too much testosterone in the air that made me uneasy. The children prattled on with their bits of news but after ten minutes they were bored and ran off to a crèche of toys in the corner. The man stood up and introduced himself as Raymonde. He thanked me for bringing the children in and said, 'The previous lady was much older than you.' Why didn't I sit down? He registered my reaction to his accent and explained he was Canadian. He had very pale blue eyes and now I took him in I saw his white hair was premature and put him in his early fifties. Straight away he volunteered that this was his second life sentence. I didn't really need to know that. He'd been paroled ten years before, he said, when he'd met the children's mother but then 'something else happened' and he found himself back inside. This wasn't how it was meant to be. I was the enabler of this visit, not its focus. What conversation could we possibly have? He offered me a cigarette with hands that shook intensely and I took one to cover up I'd noticed. In those days I smoked but had no lighter on me which meant I had to lean across the table to catch the match he held out for me. Too close. I began to feel awkward. 'You've got red hair,' he said as I sat back. I nodded. He turned to watch his children and looked sad. 'They hardly know me,' he said. 'They're very well behaved,' I said for want of anything better to say. He put his hands down flat on the table to stop them trembling. 'Are you married?' he said. I nodded again. 'Would you like to know why I got my first life sentence?' No. No. No, I wanted to shout. Instead I said, 'You don't have to,' and made a gesture of indifference. But he'd already launched himself. 'It was after the war,' he said, talking in an oddly formal, fluent way. 'I'd been demobbed and I was engaged to a young lady. In the army I'd had some training in mechanics and I was working in a garage. I could see how the motor trade was picking up just after the war and I came across this place on the Banbury road that I thought would be ideal for setting up my own place. I worked very hard and every week gave all my money to my fiancée to look after for us and our future. One day I went to call for her at her mother's house but her mother said she wasn't in. She'd gone to the park; so I went down there to find her. They were canoodling on the bandstand, her and this other man, so I went up to her and confronted her. She laughed in my face. I asked her where my money was and she laughed some more. Then she took some of my letters from her handbag and began to tear them into little pieces in front of me and I saw red. I had the knife in my back pocket. I don't know how it got there.' Stop! Stop! I wanted to shout. Looking back now there were all sorts of flaws in this account and some I knew right then but it's impossible to describe what it is like when another human being sits two feet away from you and calmly describes how he committed a murder. The man called Raymonde sat back in his chair. 'I wanted to tell you,' he said. 'I could see you'd understand.' I was shaking inside. I knew I'd been manipulated but saw no way to close the whole thing down. I was too sheltered, too hemmed in by middle-class politeness and social inhibitions to bawl him out as I would have done now. I believe he'd seen all this and worked on it.

The outcome happened five weeks later when the probation officer telephoned me sounding nervous. She told me that the prisoner, Raymonde, had had his pre-parole interview in which he'd turned down various offers of support because he said he knew a lady on the outside who was going to help him and described me in detail. Although I had given out none of my contact details I was genuinely frightened, as I think was the probation officer who knew, whether through overwork or inattention, she'd made a serious miscalculation. She had sent a youngish woman into the prison to visit a man whose previous history in relation to women she knew quite well, and now there was a situation which she was duty bound to tell me about. To be fair it all went to a higher level and was dealt with effectively and I heard no more, but that was the end of any voluntary probation work for me. I hadn't the right qualities to set the boundaries from the start and to stick to them.

After all this it was a relief to get back to the next theatre job, even though occasionally things threatened to be overwhelming there too as I juggled all the pieces of my life.

I was working at the Contact Theatre in Manchester in rehearsal for the second time with Brecht's *The Good Woman of Setzuan* and already cutting it fine because at night I was playing the litigant in

Robert Bolt's *A Man for All Seasons* back in Leeds, when a call came through for me at 4.30 one afternoon. Pamela Vezey had slipped and broken her arm in the snow, it was early March, and I was to go on that night as Alice More with script in hand. Everything was panic after that. Taxi, train, taxi. I arrived at the theatre in Leeds at 6.00 p.m. with just enough time before curtain-up to fit me into Pam's costume, and for Michael Attenborough, the associate director, to walk me through the scenes with Laurence Payne, who was playing Thomas More. It was only then I thought to ask who would be playing the litigant now in my stead? Nobody had thought about that in the drama of it all. I was told I would have to do both which resulted in the hilarious situation of me walking out of one scene as Alice More, having a dun-coloured cloak thrown on me in the wings by Art Malik in his first job, and coming straight back on in the other part. By the next night I'd learned the whole of Alice More overnight and went on without the book. This sounds very impressive but over the three-week run I'd absorbed most of the lines. What I treasured most was the note Laurence Payne, of Sexton Blake television fame, gave me on the last night. 'That wasn't an understudying. It was a fine performance. Congratulations.'

The run had ended and so had a piece of my world. My father died suddenly of a stroke while battling radiotherapy for throat cancer at the end of that winter. When the news came one early morning Jim was there for me as I had been for him, only this time he wept with me. He had grown to admire my father's wisdom and humanity, as well as his bad jokes and the respect was mutual. In the years after my marriage my father had been able to put aside his feelings about the mixed marriage and enjoy Jim's company for what it was. Their conversations were lively and wide-ranging, usually of a philosophical, intellectual bent and always ending with football. Now we were burying him in the snow that astonishingly came down that year in late April. My father's second cousin, Leslie, recited *kaddish* at the grave and there was a good turn-out of men my father had grown up with who knew him as a *mensch*. There was so much I had to thank him for; so much to emulate. His fairness and his strength, his zest and his humour, his sensitivity and above all his curiosity, which I have inherited. People interested him enormously. There was never any patronisation or prurience in his fascination in others' lives and families; always there was something to learn and respect and he was loved by his patients for it. Outside the Jewish Cemetery, the pavements were crowded with his patients who had made the four-mile trek from the deprived inner city area of his surgery to pay their respects. An old-style family doctor for most of his career, he had known many of the families over several generations and treated them with affection, producing pocket money for some of the poorest children from one pocket and lollipops from another. From him I inherited a love of music and opera, which he first introduced me to seriously when I was eleven. His method was original. He simply bought tickets for a matinee for my sister and me and told us we must make our own way to the Manchester Opera House and tell him what we thought on our return. Our first encounter was not a total success. *Madam Butterfly* from high up in the gods sung in Italian was a challenge. On the next occasion it was Verdi but by this time he made sure we had a full understanding of the synopsis beforehand. He hardly needed to, *La Traviata* thrilled us and with the Gypsy Chorus of Act II we were hooked for life. Season tickets for the Halle Orchestra under Sir John Barbirolli followed under the same principle: we must make the journey there ourselves by bus. Achievement, autonomy and trust added to the value of the experience and made it special. Concert going and opera later became an experience shared with him. I should have liked many more years of both.

He was the finest father anyone could have had and I was utterly bewildered by his death. Judith and I speak of him ever presently and appreciate his wisdom and his strength of character more and more as the years go by.

So, neither father nor father-in-law was alive shortly afterwards when Jim was appointed Registrar of the university in 1978 under the vice-chancellorship of Edward Boyle, the former minister of education in Harold Macmillan's cabinet. A brilliant man with no sense of false pride, Edward Boyle relished the role of Vice-Chancellor and took great pride in the university and in the long-established musical life of the city, quickly becoming involved with the Leeds International Piano Competition. His own musicianship was phenomenal and his friendship with Fanny Waterman and eventual chairmanship of the jury for the piano competitions was a role he valued highly. He and Jim really hit it off from the beginning and often talked politics. Jim's time in the Communist Party amused and intrigued Edward Boyle. He liked nothing more than to shock his good friend, Ted Heath, who frequently visited him in Leeds, by introducing Jim as, 'This is my Registrar, who used to sell the *Daily Worker* outside the student union.'

Edward had learned more of Jim's doings in the Communist Party on various long car journeys they had made together the previous autumn in connection with the sending down of a student for repeated exam failure. There was no need at all for Edward Boyle to go in person to explain the matter to the boy's working-class family in Nottingham but he understood exactly how many hopes would be dashed with this news and hoped his presence might soften the disappointment. This was a mark of the kind of man he was.

They went in Jim's car and whether coincidentally or by design, shortly after these journeys had taken place, Jim received a highly interesting letter one Saturday morning from the MOD (Ministry of Defence) from a man signed Parker. The envelope had an instruction that it was not to be opened other than by the addressee, and if he was abroad it was not to be forwarded but to be returned. It stated that Mr Parker (not his real name) was working on the student movement in Leeds of the early 1950s and would like to give Jim lunch at the Queen's Hotel in Leeds on a date that was convenient to him but please would he be good enough not to mention this to anyone.

With a date agreed, the lunch was held in a private dining room on the first floor of the Queen's Hotel where all conversation ceased while the waiters served the food. Mr Parker had come with a colleague and both revealed a very close knowledge of the people involved in the student movement in Leeds in the 1950s; Jim was amazed at how well they'd done their homework. What they wanted to know was if any important names had been overlooked and whether Jim had been approached while a postgraduate to work for the Soviet Union or any of its satellites, and if so by whom? Of course he hadn't but his close knowledge of the people involved in student politics prompted them to suggest a further meeting at the War Office a month later when he might have had time to recall further names.

There in the bowels of Whitehall he was faced with a wall covered in photographs and asked if he recognised any of them. Most certainly he did and was astonished by how many people had ended up on the files of MI5 or MI6. He wasn't told which of the two he was dealing with but guessed it was the latter. Briefly they discussed the student careers of those he recognised, and in some cases he was told about their subsequent history. Out of delicacy he supposed, his own photograph was not up there but the photographs of quite a few prominent Leeds citizens, pillars of the establishment were there, all of whom Jim said would have been astounded if they had known they were on file.

No further meetings took place and that was the end of the matter. Jim always suspected Edward Boyle might have given the whole thing a nudge but having sworn himself to secrecy couldn't bring it out into the open between them. If Edward did know he might well have been gently putting his tongue in cheek when he introduced Jim to Ted Heath as a former communist and watched with amusement the frisson of discomfort in his very proper friend.

A man of perfect patrician manners and shy tact, obvious status symbols passed Edward Boyle by. He dismissed the university car and driver, saying he could easily catch the bus from the vice-chancellor's lodge each day and return the same way, queuing in line with the mass of students waiting at the bus stop outside the Parkinson steps of the university. On one notable occasion during the winter of discontent, Ted Heath came up to see Edward to talk it over. An oil crisis compounded by a miners' strike had led to a three-day working week to preserve electricity: the country was in a state of unrest with compulsory electricity cuts each day throughout the country. The two friends had a private dinner in the university that evening and then, led by Boyle, walked down to the bus stop. Of course they were immediately followed by the prime minister's protection officers, who also caught the bus which found itself escorted back to Headingley by motor cycle police outriders behind and in front. What the other passengers thought when they found themselves on a bus with the prime minister, let alone what Heath thought, isn't recorded. Edward would have been oblivious which added to the piquancy of the story as it went the rounds.

The high point in the university calendar was the honorary degree ceremony held each May. A committee had been considering names for some months and there was always a degree of interest in the local press as the day came nearer. More memorable than others was 1980. That year the list included Tom Stoppard, to my delight, and Shirley Williams[1], to Jim's delight. The day was full of ceremonial and speeches, preceded by a lunch and afterwards by a formal dinner for over a hundred guests in full evening dress. There was a great sense of relief in the administration if things went off without a hitch and pride in general from the professoriate if Leeds had been seen to do it well. In the euphoria of all this, Justin Grossman, a senior reader in the sociology department and a New York Jew, bounded up just as things were breaking up and suggested we extend the night by going on to good friends of his in Headingley whom he knew Tom Stoppard would 'just love to meet'. In fact he'd already waylaid Stoppard and even now they were making their way to Justin's car. All we had to do was follow in ours. Jim had likewise waylaid his heroine, Shirley Williams, and had offered her a lift back to the university guest house. 'Brilliant! Bring her too,' Justin said. 'She'll love it.'

At near midnight a group of us found ourselves outside a Georgian terrace house set in darkness in Headingley, with Jim still talking nineteen to the dozen to Shirley Williams. In fact he had not stopped from the moment he'd handed her into the front passenger seat of our car and indicated to me to get in the back without bothering to introduce me. When the conversation somehow drifted

---

1   A British politician and academic. Originally a Labour Party Member of Parliament. She served in the Labour cabinet from 1974 to 1979 and was one of the 'Gang of Four' rebels who founded the Social Democratic Party in 1981.

on to the subject of nuclear weapons, something prompted her to say, 'Well, I can tell you this, if there was a nuclear war, the last person I'd like next to me in the trench would be an intellectual.' At this point Jim suddenly remembered me and said, 'Oh, I don't think you've met my wife, Vanessa,' and threw an arm up in the direction of the back seat. All I could do was smile, feeling acutely my disadvantage in a full-length cream evening dress that suggested I was all show without substance. By the time we arrived on the Headingley doorstep I was put-out and spoiling for a fight when we got home; Justin meanwhile was hammering away at the front door. Eventually lights went on and a hugely pregnant young woman opened the door in a dressing gown. Clearly we weren't expected but unfazed Justin took over. 'Hi, we've all come from an honorary degree dinner and thought we'd drop by. Shirley Williams and Tom Stoppard are with us and a bunch of other folk,' he said, then turning back to us all: 'Everyone this is Holly. She's a floor manager at YTV and works with Miriam Stoppard on that programme *Where There's Life.*' Her hastily dressed husband Charlie had appeared behind Holly and welcomed us in. Poor Holly shook hands with each of us as we crossed the threshold and congratulated each of us in turn on our honorary doctorate.

In the sitting room Charlie did his best to produce wine, coffee, tea. Tom Stoppard was obviously very bored. He separated himself from the social faux pas taking place around him and took up a stance against the Georgian fireplace, expecting to be lionised. I wasn't the only one who perceived this as a snub to the house, the evening and maybe the whole university. Shirley Williams, who was a charming woman, took over, delightfully covering the silences with enthusiastic compliments about the house, its furnishing, and the forthcoming event. Grateful to be rescued Justin went into overdrive. 'And Holly paints,' he said. 'Really, she's a great artist. Show us some of your paintings, Holly.' When Holly demurred not once, but twice, Justin went to the cupboard under the stairs and dragged out some large canvases and propped them up against the wall with their backs facing us. Everyone except Stoppard drifted across to look as he began to turn them the right way round. The first was a nude; the second a larger nude; the third, fourth and fifth more graphic nudes. No one knew what to say until Shirley Williams came in as the diplomat. 'Very nice,' she said. 'Tell me, do you always paint figuratively?' What Tom Stoppard thought he kept to himself.

It was earlier at this dinner, as we were leaving, that I noticed that Edward Boyle seemed to be limping and sadly he was diagnosed with prostate cancer a few months later. As he declined the heart of the university was diminished. He was held in great respect and affection by all. Jim was much involved in managing the effect of his illness on the day-to-day running of the place and much involved with Edward personally, who talked to him now as a close friend. Once again Ted Heath made a sad visit to Leeds, this time to say his goodbyes, but in the last few weeks Jim and Fanny Waterman, together with Edward's sister, Ann Gold, were the only people who were with him on a daily basis. At the very end Jim sat with him and was immensely saddened at the loss of him at only fifty-eight. The university flag stood at half-mast and after the private family funeral in East Sussex, the university held a memorial at which Jim read four lines of Anglo-Saxon verse, chosen by him to summon up Edward Boyle's very English qualities of service, strength and steadfastness.

Highe scheal tha heordra
Heorte tha chenre
Mod scheal tha mar
Thay ure maegen littlath.

Our courage shall be more resolute
Our heart shall be keener
Our spirit shall be greater
As our strength lessens.

In January there was a public memorial held at Covent Garden arranged by Fanny Waterman at which Murray Perahia played and a scholarship trust was set up in Edward Boyle's name. The university calendar moved on but Edward Boyle was still talked of with affection by those who had encountered him for a long time afterwards.

The following year I was absent from the honorary degree dinner because I was working. By now a number of people understood that when Jim attended some of these formal dinners without me, I was working in the theatre and asked with genuine interest after the particular production I was involved in. Shortly after the event I had a phone call from Mollie Jenkins, the wife of David Jenkins, the professor of theology who was shortly to be appointed the new Bishop of Durham and a good friend of Jim's. Both Mollie and David were delightful people, warm, energetic and committed to doing good in the world. Mollie had tireless energy combined with fearlessness of purpose wrapped up in a wonderfully eccentric personality. Single-handed she'd founded a school for those dropout pupils consigned to the scrapheap after mainstream education had rejected them. Now she was turning their lives around with remarkable success from a renovated building in South Leeds. Recently she'd received educational approval and some funding, but it was never enough and she was always looking for new ways to raise more. That summer she had organised a grand garden party with all the proceeds to go towards the school. Employing her usual charm and persistence, she had managed to get Merlyn Rees, the MP for Leeds South and a former Home Secretary, to open the garden party and as a further attraction also persuaded Gypsy Rose Lee, the clairvoyant from Blackpool Pier and of television fame, to come and do some fortune telling. The only problem was Gypsy Rose Lee couldn't arrive until the afternoon and so, she said, she'd thought of me. I was an actress, wasn't I? Wouldn't it be good if I came along in the morning as the spoof fortune teller and held the fort in the meantime? All in a worthwhile cause of course. There would be no end of interest and it would all help to create a general atmosphere of fun and enjoyment. How could I possibly say 'No'?

Decked out in a long, rainbow striped, hessian skirt and gypsy hoop earrings with a red scarf on my head and several medallions round my neck, I turned up in a large garden in North Leeds on a Saturday in July. Rain was already threatened and Mollie was distractedly running about with her arms flapping in all directions. I tried to tell her I'd arrived, and to have her reassurance that she'd announce me as the spoof fortune teller but she just said, 'Yes dear. In a minute. We're about to start,' and dashed back to the mock stage where she tapped the microphone to signal to the eager crowd in front that proceedings were under way. First she welcomed them all enthusiastically and then pushed Merlyn Rees forward, 'a man who needs no introduction from me and whom we are enormously thrilled to have here to pronounce this garden party open.' Merlyn Rees took the microphone from her to say a few standard things about being delighted to be there and to praise the work of Mollie's school and then handed the microphone back just as the heavens opened and the tannoy system started to falter. In a series of loud booms and inaudible hisses Mollie tried to promote all the fun on offer: the tombola; the cake stall; the white elephant stall; the flower arrangement competition; the coconut shy and of course the famous Gypsy Rose Lee from television. I waited and waited for the next announcement about my spoof impersonation but it never happened. Instead a loud clap of thunder announced the worst and everyone ran to take cover under the several marquees dotted about. I ran too, after Mollie. 'You never said anything,' I panted as I came up to her. 'Oh it will be all right dear,' she said. 'There's a notice outside your tent over there that says it's just 50 pence for you. It's a pound for the real thing when she arrives this afternoon. Now how are you going to do it? Do you want a crystal ball because we've got one for you or will you do it with tea leaves? One of these nice girl helpers just here will bring you what you want so do hurry along there.' I was out of my depth already and Mollie had turned away to attend to something else. I looked at the schoolgirl helper beside me and mumbled tea leaves would do. Goodness knows what one did with a crystal ball and, doing as I was bid, I walked towards the tent Mollie had pointed out to me. In front of it, a giant display board held an enormous publicity photograph of Gypsy Rose Lee in a rose-pink tailored suit and stud earrings. Mistake number one I thought as my medallions clanked against my heaving bosom.

Inside the tent was a card table covered in a red velvet cloth with two chairs either side of it. When the tea leaves arrived they came in the form of a large, catering size, aluminium teapot on a battered tray alongside two thick white mugs. One could have been forgiven for thinking this was really some rather crude tea party put together in a hurry. I'd little time to think about it at all though because just then the tent flap opened and in walked Merlyn Rees. We stared at each other for a few seconds like two goldfish before he started speaking. 'Good morning,' he said rubbing his hands together shyly.

'I've never done anything like this before but always wondered how it's done.' With horror I realised he thought I was the real thing, and had set himself up to be a good sport and enter into the spirit of the day with all it had on offer. In a flash I realised I could only disabuse him at the cost of his loss of dignity and extreme embarrassment. I grabbed the teapot and looked heavenwards for inspiration. This required every ounce of creative ingenuity I'd ever conjured up in any improvisation in any theatre workshop ever. 'Well,' I said, 'I read the tea leaves and what I want you to do is to pour out a mug of tea and then empty half of it on to the grass.' 'Oh yes,' he said and followed my instructions carefully, setting the mug down on the tray between us when he'd finished. Together we peered at the mess of tea leaves climbing the side of the mug. Help! Help! I wanted to say and gave a dramatic pause as I stared down into it. 'Ah!' I said meaningfully and then 'Ah!' again. 'This is very interesting. I see the number four has been very important in your life.' Where had I got that from? He sat back in his chair shaking his head. 'That's remarkable,' he said with growing excitement. 'The number four is indeed significant for me. 'I joined the RAF in 1941, Colleen and I were married in 1949 and our house was number 42. In 1964 I was appointed parliamentary secretary to James Callaghan and in 1974 I was appointed secretary of state for Northern Ireland.' I'd found the secret! This was how it was done. You let people tell their own fortunes. Everyone wants to hear only good things about themselves. Flushed with my success I leaned forward again and said, 'Now you see how this column of tea leaves is climbing towards the rim?' 'Yes,' he said agreeing with me. 'Oh, yes.' 'Well this suggests to me,' I said, 'that the best is yet to come. You will climb higher still. Even bigger success is written for you.' This was naughty of me but irresistible. Michael Foot was still leader of the Labour Party and not doing well and hope springs eternal in the human breast, or it did in the breast in front of me. Merlyn Rees blushed pink and wiped his nose on his handkerchief. 'Truly remarkable,' he said. 'Truly. I'll never be a sceptic again. In fact I'm going to find Colleen right now and tell her she needs to come in here and have her own fortune told.' And with that he got up and thanked me profusely. I walked with him to the tent flap and saw a line of people outside, all waving their tickets at me. 'I'm next,' one of them shouted out. 'No, it's me,' another said. Most of them had their shopping baskets at their feet. They'd come up from Leeds Market with their cauliflowers and cabbages determined not to miss their turn with a television celebrity. But by now I was calm. And so it went on all morning. I supplied the number, a magic three or six or seven. It didn't really matter; the enquirer did all the rest. For two hours the formula worked like a dream. Perhaps I had an alternative career but I wasn't going to put it to the test any time soon.

In 1984 Jim and I were in York Minster to see David Jenkins's inauguration as the new Bishop of Durham in a sumptuous, ancient pageant of dignity and ritual. Unfortunately, David had already attracted the wrong publicity when he had done an in-depth interview on television in which he said he didn't believe in the literal truth of the Virgin birth: views he might have expressed in the senior common room of any university but on such a public platform they had offended and gleaned him a lot of unfair opprobrium. There was real opposition made to his appointment with a petition of 12 000 names submitted to the Archbishop of York. Halfway through the inauguration, an impassioned vicar climbed the pulpit steps and shouted out in sincere distress, 'This is blasphemy to our Lord.' He was seized by the cathedral's security officers but resisted removal by clinging on to the lectern with both hands and continuing to rail against the proceedings. At which point the panoply of magnificently clad bishops and senior churchmen cried out jointly and severally, 'Shame! Shame! Shame!' Three days later the roof of the minster was struck by lightning resulting in a disastrous fire, which many interpreted as an act of God. After the ceremony, Jim and I were in the group of people, led by David, making our way to private reception rooms at the back of the minster when a journalist thrust a microphone at David and asked him what he was going to do next. He replied, 'I think like Brer Rabbit, I'll just lie low for a bit', perhaps not the wisest response. He and Mollie were truly good people, who became identified with opposition to Thatcher's policies. His stance on the Miners' Strike and other important issues earned him the tag of the Red Bishop as a term of censure, a term that failed to describe his humanity and compassionate Christianity.

It was during the Miners' Strike that I had the small part of a concerned parent in David Hare's film *Wetherby* which was being filmed on location in South Yorkshire. Vanessa Redgrave was in the lead as a schoolteacher, Jean Travers, and my short scene was with her. It is difficult to sum up star quality. There is no single attribute that can define it; those incredible light blue eyes, the voice, the manner, the bearing, all make up a charisma that's unforgettable. For many, her extreme left-wing politics are hard to take, but her luminosity and her beauty forgive all.

My cameo scene involved me and my film husband consulting our daughter's teacher, Jean Travers, on parents' night. We stood in a tight triangle in the school hall as various camera set-ups were being configured, me beside Vanessa Redgrave. The floor manager was busy listening to the director's instructions coming down through his head cans and repeating them out loud as, 'Vanessa, darling, could you step a little more to the left. To the right. Back. Forwards.' Obligingly I stepped left, stepped right, back and forwards until a voice called out,

'Whoa!' After a hiatus the floor manager approached me looking exasperated. 'Have you got another name?' he asked. 'Yes. Susan,' I mumbled, a name I've always disliked. Vanessa Redgrave smiled off into the distance. 'Right. For today you're Susan,' he said and walked off. Eventually the director appeared, none other than David Hare himself, to apologise to his star in person for his crassness in putting me in the scene. How do you get over your existence being dismissed? This was an uncomfortable reminder of my very first voice class at Central. Then, Clifford Turner, one of my tutors, told me they had had another Vanessa at Central before me, who also had the same V R initials as myself and I had 'a lot to live up to'.

As is usual in film, all the scenes in the school hall were being shot on the same day with lots of boys and girls milling around, supposedly in rehearsal for the school play, *A Man for All Seasons*. When Vanessa Redgrave heard that the boy playing the boatman was a miner's son, which signalled to her large-scale deprivation and starvation, she sprang into action, marching him off to the mobile catering unit every hour to feed him up. He was, to start with, a round-faced young boy and it reached the point when he was dodging behind pillars to avoid her, holding on to his tummy to mime his discomfort to the rest of us. I had already been part of a loose group she had addressed in a tea break in impassioned tones, telling us that workers of the world needed to unite to overthrow world capitalism. It sounded like something she'd learned by rote. Behind her back a grips boy went past holding his nose and pulling an imaginary lavatory chain.

Most of the extras on the film were turns from the many working men's clubs in the area. *Daily Mail* readers one and all, who sat around at lunchtime loudly praising Thatcher and her policies, until Vanessa Redgrave wafted up to them clutching an armful of WRP

(Workers Revolutionary Party) newspapers and after apologising profusely for interrupting their lunch, asked if they would buy one to support the miners' cause. Faced with that beautiful smile and in awe of her fame the men simply melted. To a man, they dug into their pockets for loose change. Only after she'd left did they look at each other shamefacedly, before resuming their barroom politics. She was simply irresistible.

Professional change for me had begun at the start of the decade. With the girls coming up to thirteen and eleven, I had begun to consider working further afield and when I was offered the pre-Christmas show at Alan Ayckbourn's Theatre in the Round at Scarborough I moved into digs. Out of season this meant a small flat with a lacquered brown wood sideboard and a faux leather three-piece suite. I was a great admirer of Ayckbourn and only sorry I wasn't going there to do one of his plays. This was my first experience of working in theatre in the round. From the start I enjoyed the immediate sense of contact with the audience but learning where to be on stage took longer. Only standing parallel to the three tunnel passages on to the stage called 'voms', or vomitoriums to give them their full name, taken from the architecture of the Roman amphitheatre, was one sure of not giving one's back to a section of the audience; of course there were occasions when this was unavoidable and I watched some telling 'back' acting in others' performances. It was strange being in 'digs' once more and stranger still playing host to my own daughters when I had them over for tea after they'd been to see a matinee. All of a sudden Mum was in a strange kitchen with a Formica-topped table and unfamiliar crockery. We were all oddly shy. The wind off the North Sea rattled the ill-fitting windows and my memory tells me that it was driving rain most days. I was in a café sheltering from yet another squall when I heard the news that

John Lennon had been shot outside the Dakota building in New York: the end of another era. Miniskirts and madness, kipper ties and flares, and his music above everything else that will always take me back to my youth and the careless optimism of it all. The eighties had arrived with an aggressive thrust and its own tunes that seemed to be only ever about money, money, money: that golden key to the sunny uplands of the super rich. I'm all right, Jack and who gives a hoot for the rest?

Chapter 7

EASTERN EUROPE

We were going to Poland to represent Leeds University at a distinguished ceremony to celebrate the fortieth anniversary of the setting up of Lodz Technica Universitat in 1945. Jerzy Kroh, the rector of Lodz, had gained his PhD in textiles at Leeds in the 1950s under Sir Fredrick Dainton and the relationship that had then begun between the textile departments of both universities had been fostered and actively encouraged on both sides. The Vice-Chancellor of Leeds was unavailable, being at the Commonwealth Universities Conference in Sydney, and had asked Jim to go in his place. So, there I was, returning on a British Airways Boeing 737 jet to the land my grandparents had left over a hundred years before. As we descended the steps from the aircraft in Warsaw I was overcome with emotion and had a sudden impulse to kiss the ground: a ludicrous gesture mercifully thwarted by the presence of Russian soldiers armed with Kalashnikovs awaiting us on the tarmac. In any case it wasn't the land I wanted to pay homage to but to my roots there in that soil. Once upon a time, a long, long time ago, and for generation upon generation before that, I had sprung from this country, or a part of me had. Would I find here an off-the-peg identity I could put on and wear with immediate effect to solve my problems of belonging?

It was 1985 and the Soviet stamp was on everything. The city was without colour and closed in on itself. Few people walked the pavements and those that did appeared to be hurrying to some urgent destination. Shops were indistinguishable from other buildings, without advertising or awnings it was difficult to make them out. Near the hotel the blackened walls of former textile mills hung over both sides of the street to form a dark canyon of gloom. The marble steps up to the hotel itself were pitted and worn; inside, the foyer was dominated by a once elaborate rococo staircase dripping with chipped gold plaster ornamentation under a tired chandelier. The same rococo decoration continued in the bedroom with its high ceiling and carved gold headboards. In its glory days, this must have been a fashionable hotel. Twin beds with satin covers faced twin washbasins, side by side. I had seen and knew well the harrowing photographs that Henryk Ross filmed secretly of the Lodz ghetto and which he produced as evidence at the Eichmann trial. They were vivid in my head as I now made an awful connection. This hotel, the best in town during the war years, would have been where SS officers were billeted before the final liquidation of the ghetto in January 1945. In this very room two SS officers might have lounged with Brylcreemed heads against these same gold headboards the night before the *aktion*, shaved at the twin washbasins on the morning itself. I shivered in the horror of the picture I'd conjured up. What was forty years in the scheme of things? We had come to celebrate a beginning and yet everything around me reminded me simultaneously of an ending and annihilation. The irony was stark and multiplied for me over the following two days when the partying began.

The next day, in contrast to the drabness all around, the honorary degree ceremony was a blaze of colour and medieval ritual. The academic dress of the distinguished participants was a mass of crimson, gold and turquoise, worn with ermine capes of great luxuriousness. Instead of plain mortars, the academic headgear consisted of ornate velvet caps in many different colours, reminiscent of court jesters. Taken as a whole it was like looking at a re-enacted Holbein painting and as the great pageant of the senior academic staff of Lodz processed towards the dais, accompanied by Russian martial music; the sheer theatricality of it all was impressive. Only the Russian generals in full dress uniform, guns at their side, struck an incongruous note. Down in the body of the hall distinguished guests did their best to match the sartorial elegance on display above them but apart from us and one other couple from Strathclyde University, there were no representatives from the West. East Germany, Cuba, Bulgaria, Yugoslavia, Nicaragua and Czechoslovakia were all well represented in ill-fitting suits and old-fashioned dresses. Jerzy Kroh, as rector, made the first speech, which he translated roughly into English for the benefit of those of us without Polish. It was to the effect that out of the ashes and devastation of 1945 a great research university had been born on the site of a former factory. This was met with thunderous applause by the audience and by me with unease. Wasn't I conniving at some gross denial by bringing my hands together like the rest? Outside this building there were different ashes. No one was talking about them. Whose factory? Who owned it? Worked in it? It was like being in 'Looking Glass Land' without any restorative. I should be putting up my hand to be counted, but as what? Instead I sat through speech after speech and behaved politely. Now it was the turn of the Russian generals. Several of them made speeches and several of them appeared to be getting honorary doctorates. For what? Subjugation? Censorship? Intimidation? As an example in sycophancy it couldn't have been clearer. After less than twenty-four hours in Poland, Jim and I had already learned how intensely the Russians were disliked, right down to re-naming vodka as Polish gin.

After the honorary degree ceremony we adjourned to a reception in the rector's official residence, where all the foreign representatives, including me, were presented with a commemorative medal to mark our presence at this auspicious occasion. A vague guilt settled on me. Here I was being feted and fussed over and out there were the traces of a Jewish history I was unequivocally part of. I should be making amends but to whom? Mrs Vanessa, as they called me when they bowed with exquisite Polish courtesy to kiss my hand, was an imposter who had come to bear witness to an altogether different history.

In the evening the British Council threw their own party as part of good international relations. At the pre-dinner drinks an immense twittering started up amongst the Polish academic wives as if a flock of excitable birds had landed in the hall. I asked the wife of a British Council representative what they were whispering about and she told me they were whispering that iced cakes were being served later. And there indeed they were when we reached the coffee stage, 'Mr Kipling'-like cakes in lurid colours of pink and orange and mauve and coffee, each with a jelly sweet on top. I pretended not to notice as these sedate matrons opened evening bags and tried to cram in as many of the little cakes as they could: sugared treats for party goody bags. Nothing conveyed the hardness of their lives as graphically as this sad pantomime.

Everywhere we went there was this sense of danger, of lives lived carefully to avoid attracting attention. Another incident from the previous day had brought this vividly home to me. On our first night in the hotel a tatty cabaret was put on for us in the dining room. A succession of mediocre dancers in shiny satin and a lot of make-up, twirled veils about before sashaying down to their sequinned bras and pants as a man from the three-piece band obligingly clashed the cymbals to signal an erotic climax that was absent. The dancers were followed by a magician with a white rabbit and two tumblers. All of it a pastiche of what I imagined the real thing would have been like in 1930s Berlin. There weren't enough of us to even supply a decent round of applause at the end and our chief reaction was one of embarrassment. Better to escape to the hotel bar in the basement.

Jim sat up on a bar stool and I indicated I'd join him when I returned from the ladies' cloakroom. In my brief absence I saw a woman had hoisted herself up beside him. Like the dancers she wore a lot of make-up, bright blue eye shadow and scarlet lipstick. Her low plunged blouse showed a lot of cleavage but the allure finished there. The thin black skirt was shiny with wear and her flat shoes down at heel. The total effect was a sad attempt on little money to announce her wares. I caught Jim's eyes and saw his amusement at being the target of her advances. He'd already bought her a drink and now airily waved an arm in my direction to introduce me as his wife before turning to talk to Graham Hills on his other side, the Vice-Chancellor of Strathclyde and the only other Western man in the hotel. As far as he was concerned I would deal with her now.

To give the woman her due she recovered herself quickly on finding there was a wife and introduced herself to me in good English as Anka. I could see that her first drink had disappeared and ordered her another on our tab. Her thanks were over-profuse, telling me over and over again I was a kind lady, with a kind face and then she started to cry. She told me she worked in a factory and had a little boy and needed help. Twelve years before some British engineers were working on a twelve-month contract in Lodz and she had met Tommy who was the father of her child and they loved each other. After his contract expired they wrote to each other. He had wanted her to go to Warsaw and get a visitor's visa for England for herself and the boy. She'd queued all day but been turned away. What could she do? Now Tommy's letters to her had stopped and she feared her own letters to him were not getting through. Would I, kind lady that I was, take her letters and post them in England? She could bring them to me the next morning and wait for me in the hotel foyer. It was only a small thing she was asking me but she was so very afraid that Tommy, who was twenty years older than her, might even no longer be alive. Her son might never know his father. Her crying started up again even louder and I almost joined in, moved by her wretchedness. Jim had turned round to hear the tail end of her story. She scrabbled for a handkerchief, clutching my hand. 'Thank you. Thank you,' she said. 'I must go now. My little boy is on his own, but I know you are a kind lady.'

'What was that about?' Jim wanted to know. I told him the gist of Anka's story and of her difficulties. He shrugged and said, 'Keep away from it' before turning back to Graham Hills. I did not tell him that I had agreed to meet Anka the next morning. I was on a mission of compassion to help the downtrodden of Eastern Europe suffering unimaginably under the Soviet yoke, and this was my own adventure.

Or so I thought when I left the breakfast room on some pretext early the next morning to wait in the foyer for Anka. Jim came across me as he headed for the lift and his face showed immediately how angry he was. He pulled me out of the armchair I was sitting in and pushed me towards the lift. As soon as its doors closed he told me how utterly stupid I was. Didn't I realise this was some kind of sting? First she'd tried to pick him up and then when that was going nowhere, turned to me. I was so naive, he said. The perfect target. Did I never question why someone who allegedly worked in a factory could speak such good English? She was crying, I said. She has a little boy. 'Oh yes!' Jim said, 'and tomorrow she'll have triplets. You're not fit to be let loose.' If this was supposed to expose her as fake, I wasn't going to accept it just like that. 'So why did she target you then?' I demanded. 'Go on tell me that?' 'How do I know?' said Jim. 'But they'll know all about my past here. If they could have compromised me in a honey-trap, that would have been a real success. Failing that a photograph of my wife accepting letters clandestinely would do as a second best.'

After that I was silent, and yes, contrite. But there was another truth behind it if Jim was right, and I realised he probably was. Unless Anka was a very good actress I'd picked up waves of hopelessness and desperation off her. What in her life had forced her into the role of stooge in the blackmail games of her masters? What might she lose if she didn't comply? Behind the surface welcome we'd received was another Eastern Europe of smoke and mirrors.

The next day we were taken on a walking tour of the town in pouring rain led by a Professor Tessmer. It was impossible for him to omit the contribution the former Jewish population had made to the city. Before 1939 the Jews of Lodz had numbered 233 000 and made up one third of its inhabitants. They had lived and worshipped in the city, been born here, married here, worked in its mills, toiled in its tailoring shops, taught in its schools, practised medicine, the law and now, it was as if they had never been. All the facts and figures of the deportations were mechanically cited by Professor Tessmer, as if he was embarrassed; he probably was. He dug his hands into his raincoat pockets and looked up at the sky while we stood under large umbrellas and looked out over the vast area that had once been the ghetto. One hundred and sixty-four thousand people had been crammed into its four square kilometres he told us. The group shifted uncomfortably as he was speaking, waiting for permission to move on but my question from the back of the group held us there temporarily. 'How many of the Lodz Jews survived the Holocaust?' I asked. Several people at the front turned round to look at me. Was it my tone or my expression? I'd identified myself as Jewish which unconsciously I had wanted to do from the beginning. 'About 900,' he said. Caught between good manners to my hosts and the rest, I nevertheless ploughed on. 'And how many Jews live here now?' I asked. We both knew the answer was a handful if that. The Polish anti-Semitism of the mid-1960s saw many survivors actively encouraged to emigrate to Israel. For the first time my connection with the numbers felt personal. Why had I never made it before? If my grandparents came from Poland, they had not sprung newly forth. Somewhere in the North East of this country there were remnants of my extended family and one day I'd find out more.

For the present, after four days of intense incident, I had had enough and even welcomed our return as the understandable anticlimax it would be; only it wasn't. The plane waited and waited on the tarmac at Warsaw Airport and I grew impatient. 'What are we waiting for?' I asked. The plane was fully boarded. We were bang on schedule. 'It will be some VIP,' Jim said. And sure enough, after several minutes a black Mercedes started to make its way the ludicrously short distance from the terminal building to the foot of the aircraft steps. The rear car door opened and Robert Maxwell stepped out, followed by his aide, a browbeaten Sir Tom McCaffrey. I started to point them out to Jim; I didn't need to. He put his hand over my raised arm to bring it down and said from the side of his mouth. 'Don't look now. Just carry on reading.' I looked at him. He'd picked up his own book again. Ah! We were playing some game. Was that it? Amused I picked up my own book but from the corner of one eye, I caught Maxwell's entry on board and saw him look around to see what kind of a stir he had created. There was none, the only other passenger in business class besides ourselves was a woman on her own. Escorted to his seat by the stewardess, he flung himself down in the row parallel to us across the aisle. Sir Tom was sent to sit behind him. Next he proceeded to take off his shoes and sling them down the aisle and then to push his feet forwards into the empty seat beside the poor woman in front of him. He glanced around again; no one was looking at him. We were reading. The aircraft door was shut and we taxied down the runway.

As soon as the seat belt sign went off, Maxwell called up the air stewardess and asked for a glass of champagne and equally immediately sent it back because he said it was, 'Like warm horse piss.' Instead he asked for a beer, then called the air stewardess back to say, 'And I want your pilot to call up the television mast in Norway and find out how my team, Oxford United, are doing.' Off she went once more and Maxwell picked up his newspaper. Only as the plane levelled out did Jim lean across the aisle to tap Maxwell on the shoulder and ask him with a twinkle if he was plotting the downfall of Eddie Shah. The great head reared round and the great mouth roared, 'Eddie Shah! I'm not plotting any downfall of Eddie Shah: he'll ruin himself in six months.' (Eddie Shah was about to launch his technologically advanced newspaper *Today*.) Then he caught up with himself and turned the scrutiny on Jim. 'Who are you?' he demanded, 'and what were you doing in Warsaw with your good lady?' Jim explained about the reciprocal arrangement between the two universities and Maxwell offered in return that he had been in Warsaw interviewing General Jaruzelski. I think we were meant to be impressed; we didn't show it. Maxwell went back to his newspaper for a while and then began talking about universities in general and the disasters he said were being wrought in them by the policies of Mrs Thatcher. In fact he said he was trying to get a few people together to do something about it but saw the biggest obstacles to progress as the vice-chancellors themselves. Jim didn't disagree with that, which Maxwell seemed to like. What did we think about Leeds in general then, he wanted to know. 'I own half the shops there,' he said boastfully. 'Really,' Jim said. 'We always do our shopping in Manchester.' It was a case of touché! Maxwell roared with laughter before agreeing that the shops were pretty awful and he was proposing to do something about them. 'In about ten years' time Leeds will be buzzing,' he said. (He was to be right about that.) He was still smiling as he returned to his newspaper but from time to time cast a shrewd eye in Jim's direction, obviously he liked people who stood up to him. For his part, Jim just sucked in his cheeks and pursed his lips as he stared ahead at nothing, a sign I knew well that he was thinking about something. When he slightly turned in his seat to speak to Maxwell next, his tone was considered. If Maxwell had so many interests in Leeds, Jim said, perhaps Maxwell should think about becoming a member of the court of Leeds University which was a mechanism and a symbol of the university's accountability to the wider local community? Maxwell seemed genuinely surprised and then flattered. He looked out of the plane window and thought a minute and then said simply if Leeds wanted that, he'd be willing. The matter having been settled, he pulled out an enormous Cuban cigar, and waved it at the 'No Smoking' sign. Did we mind? 'A sex symbol is a sex symbol, but a good cigar is a smoke,' Jim said quoting Groucho Marx. Maxwell laughed some more and threw the joke back to Sir Tom McCaffray behind him as he lit up.

Just as we were about to land at Heathrow he turned to Jim again and said in a revealing moment, 'If your vice-chancellor doesn't think I'm a fit and proper person to be on the university court, I shall quite understand.' But Maxwell was elected to the court and the story of Jim recruiting him on the Warsaw flight went round the university. There then followed a business liaison that was entirely in keeping with Maxwell's reputation. After several visits to the university with Kevin Maxwell in tow, arriving each time by private helicopter that landed on the university sports fields to the puzzlement of the many students there, he set up the Maxwell Chemistry Institute to the tune of £4.5 million together with another enterprise. He had correctly judged the need for the universities to enter into commercial partnerships for their future survival and Jim had correctly judged that for all Maxwell's vast sphere of influence and success, he lacked the veneer of respectability that the relationship with a major civic university like Leeds gave him; or gave him until he disappeared off the side of a yacht into the shark-infested waters around the Canary Islands and with him disappeared the remaining promised, but as yet unpaid, £1.5 million.

The following year the nuclear reactor at Chernobyl exploded putting in peril the lives of thousands of men, women and children through radiation exposure. This was the Ukraine, not Poland, but I could picture the bewildered faces of the kinds of people I'd met who lived under the Soviet banner, people like Anka and Professor Tessmer from the walking tour. Men and women bred to obey the rules without question. In spite of the Soviet Union's attempt to contain information about the scale of the disaster, bits of news trickled through to the West. The whole of the city of Pripyat, some 50000 people, were forcibly evacuated. Pictures of them boarding trains came through on television, most of them looking traumatised by the cataclysmic event that had occurred on their doorstep. Torn overnight from their homes and their livelihoods, they were told to abandon their family pets because of the risk of radioactive contamination. As much as anything the callousness of the Soviet mindset was captured for me in the images of hundreds of these dogs running piteously after their families only to be shooed away. Surely a shooting would have been more humane than starvation and disease? Men, women, children and now animals were just numbers in the general Soviet indifference to individual suffering.

Eastern Europe fascinated and repelled me in equal measure: I wanted to understand more. My visit to Lodz was the first of what would turn out to be six trips I would make to Eastern Europe over the next twenty years but the only trip I experienced in the Soviet era. I was glad of the experience because it gave me a yardstick with which to measure the changes that followed after the collapse of the Berlin Wall. In Prague in 1996 the advances towards capitalism were so rapid one felt the designer boutiques had been waiting in the wings for years, only to be wheeled out when the timing was ripe.

But I couldn't forget the abandoned dogs of Chernobyl, though for a long time I could do nothing about it – nor indeed heard anything. Not until nearly three decades later did I discover an American charity I could support, founded to help the descendants of those abandoned animals. Somehow the poor creatures had survived on scraps of vegetation and the prey they'd managed to scavenge in the wild. Their greatest threat had come not from radiation, but from the starvation they'd endured and from the harshness of the Ukrainian winters.

Growing up we'd always had a family dog. Any life without a dog would have been unthinkable to my mother. In her devotion to animals, I nearly had the full description of her girlhood and growing up. Something a bit tomboyish, always outdoors, land, open spaces, animals; dogs, cats, her pet goose. Her four first cousins on her mother's side were all farmers, none of which I knew until after she died. In the countryside she was confident and relaxed. And yet her style and dress sense as a city wife and mother showed flair and distinction. Tall, slim with what my father always called her 'good deportment', she cut an attractive figure. Within the home she was the policymaker, even slightly grande dame, a side of her that could show itself in restaurants and dress shops as a kind of '*de haut en bas*' which made me cringe. But she was a loving and demonstrative mother in my early childhood. Later, I felt her approval of me was conditional and I strove hard to please her. Her values, of fairness, decency and patriotism, were Lancashire values she shared with Jim, which should have made them get on but didn't. All of it was too close to home for her. She'd moved on from all of that into something more evolved and in her eyes, Jim's family background of operatives in the cotton mills was lower down the tree than her yeoman farmer forebears of whom she was proud. Linking them together as fellow Lancastrians denied her the edge. On the surface there was a veneer of affability and politeness between them but neither made a real effort to know the other and I was caught in the middle.

Outside the home, in contrast, she could be shy in large gatherings of my father's friends, many of whom had grown up with him in Cheetham Hill and whose families were interconnected. They saw her as gentle, even self-effacing. On those occasions I saw it too and, early on, puzzled how she could be two different personalities. With maturity I understood her diffidence. The remnants of my father's family had always maintained a distant, dutiful connection with her and, now that he was gone, this dwindled even more. I ached for a brave loneliness that had crept into her now and seemed to lap at her confidence as she entered her eightieth year. She was a woman of worth and decency and it made me angry that they could not value her for herself alone. In certain quarters she would always be the category of *shiksa* and I had long ago taken on some of her pain as my own.

No one examines this better than Arthur Miller in his play *A View from the Bridge*. Through inappropriate feelings for his niece and jealousy of her moving away from him, Eddie Carbone betrays his relative Marco to the immigration authorities as an illegal immigrant. Before his arrest and deportation, Marco comes looking for him and calls him an animal. In torment, Eddie cries out 'I want my name, Marco. Now give me my name.' He means recognise me and respect me for myself, as a flawed man, not as a category. Around the time of my mother's eightieth birthday, I was playing Beatrice, Eddie Carbone's wife, at the Everyman Theatre in Cheltenham and heard in those words, every night, some parallels with my mother's long journey as my father's wife. Beatrice can't alter the tragic outcome for Eddie Carbone ordained in the play and I couldn't alter the unkind generic categorisation of my mother. I wanted her to see the show, wondering if she would receive the lines in anything like the same way as I did but self-analysis wasn't a part of her make-up. She couldn't intellectualise her part in her own story to give it context.

Instead the whole weekend was a little adventure for her. I knew Cheltenham would be a place that would tick a lot of her boxes and booked her into a nice hotel in Montpellier from where she could enjoy pottering in the antique shops and dress shops round about. The weather in January wasn't the best but it was nice to see her enjoying herself. She bought a pale lilac mohair coat in Cavendish House, the department store on the promenade, and it so perfectly suited her fading prettiness that whenever I think of her, I see her in that coat. In any case I had my own problems with the production as the run went on.

As a drama student I was obsessed with Brecht and thought his style of theatre in which artifice was banished and actors sat on chairs throughout the play, standing to enter a scene only when their character came into the action, was exciting. This is just representation, we were saying. We are merely actors taking on parts. Here before you is a human dilemma that must be resolved by us and by you the audience in a joint emotional collaboration. But from my first encounter of working in an Arthur Miller play I had replaced Brecht with Arthur Miller as my number one playwright. I was thrilled to have the chance of working in *A View from the Bridge* and had been looking forward to the production.

It didn't work out entirely as I'd hoped. The Australian actor who played opposite me as Eddie Carbone had trained as a method actor. It was the first time I'd come across the fruits of such a purist form of training and, on the nights when Eddie stopped speaking altogether or put his head in his hands because he said 'that was how Eddie was feeling at the time', I was thrown. But on the night that he suddenly picked up the kitchen table in both hands and hurled it towards Abigail Thaw, playing his niece Catherine, and myself because, he said, 'Eddie felt angrier than usual', we both decided to keep as far away from him on stage as possible. He ended up in the show report for that, but it made little difference. Every night became a roller-coaster of challenges and I formed my own view of method acting as selfish, and even began to wish the run would be over so that the next show I was there to do, Michael Frayn's *Noises Off* could come into production.

The Everyman Theatre, Cheltenham, is a beautiful Frank

Matcham theatre, seating nearly 700, which entirely suits its setting in that stylish Georgian town. The auditorium matches every child's idea of theatre, with a gilded proscenium arch, red velvet curtains, a magnificent ceiling, and elegant dress and upper circles that curve out in gracious lines above the stalls. The acoustics are perfect, better than many modern theatres. I'd been there the previous summer doing Alan Ayckbourn's *A Chorus of Disapproval*. That too was memorable, though not necessarily for the right reason.

A Chorus of Disapproval is a joyous, company play set in a Northern Amateur operatic society that is in rehearsal for John Gay's *The Beggar's Opera*. Everything that can go wrong seemingly does go wrong but here, life proved stranger than fiction.

On the first Thursday matinee, the actress playing Rebecca Huntley-Pike, the bossy, upper-class character, the matriarch of the am-dram society, forgot all about the matinee, and having come in to collect her wages, Thursday being pay-day, wandered off to sunbathe in the park. Her absence wasn't discovered until after the half-hour call. Back then no one had mobile phones, so various ASMs were sent off to search the town frantically for her, all to no avail. Hastily, we were summoned by Jenny, the DSM (Deputy Stage Manager), just before curtain-up. She told us to keep calm and carry on as usual. This first act was an ensemble piece with the whole company on stage; no one would notice the absence of one character if Vanessa took over Rebecca Huntley-Pike's lines, thus ensuring no cue lines were lost. In the meantime Jenny would work out a contingency plan for the next two acts.

It was never going to work. Rebecca Huntley-Pike's lines, crafted by a master like Ayckbourn, expressed her character's hauteur and arrogance to perfection. Clearly they didn't suit my character of Enid Washbrook, a timorous, mousey woman. I tried hard to say Rebecca's line of outraged complaint, 'We've all been sitting back there in the cold for two-and-a-half hours', in a timorous, mousey voice but all that came out of me were high register squeaks. Someone in the company started to giggle. Then there was a snort from somewhere else. My next Rebecca line meant running her question and my Enid Washbrook reply into one speech, which didn't make sense and by now other actors were openly corpsing. It took off like wildfire, as it always does, and very soon we were all convulsed to the point of shaking as we tried to control ourselves. On stage it was chaos as the company edged towards group hysteria and in the auditorium it was bewilderment as the audience tried to make out what was going on. I could see Jenny in the wings frantically miming that she was about to bring the curtain down on us. There is a dimension of fear in corpsing on that scale, almost of transgression, as if one is demolishing the fourth wall with one's bare hands. Stagecraft is discipline and we'd abandoned ours to have our own party up there on stage while the audience had paid money to see Ayckbourn's play. For such offence we all ended up in the show report with me, on this occasion, as chief culprit, which seemed a little unfair.

In the second and third acts a theatre administrator was hauled up from her office to go on with the book. The poor, absent actress herself walked nonchalantly into the backstage corridor as we were gathering in full eighteenth-century costumes and wigs to go on stage to do the finale, a chorus number from John Gay's opera. The look of horror on her face was a snapshot of every actor's nightmare.

Living in Cheltenham for three months was fortunate in that it placed me near Nerissa at secretarial college in Oxford, with her sights set on a Mountbatten internship to New York the following year, and Emilia at university in Bristol. I had brought Sam, the six-year-old border collie, with me and, on weekends when Jim was down, we were complete as a family in Gloucestershire and Sam could round us all up to his great delight.

Of all the dogs in my life up until then Sam was the star and we were devoted to each other. The rapport between him and me was extra special. He was exuberant when I was, quiet and thoughtful when I was down in spirits, endlessly affectionate and fiercely loyal to me. Left at home in the now empty nest, he would have pined. I was fortunate in my digs in the basement of the Powells' beautiful Georgian house, where I had the run of what would have been the below stairs kitchens, now transformed into a large bedsitting room. The French windows opened on to a yard where steps led up to the garden making it ideal for Sam. All the rules from home were suspended in this new environment and he slept on my bed in total heaven. In the mornings I took him for long walks in Pittville Park before going into rehearsal where he was as good as gold. The only problem I had with him came the first time I had him in the dressing room during a performance of *Noises Off* in which I was playing Dotty Otley. As soon as he heard my voice over the tannoy, answered by what he took to be an aggressive male voice, he sprang to my defence and barked his head off. After that he was relegated to the stage door, well away from the dressing rooms and the tannoy, but came into his own in the bar after the show where he was fussed over, fed crisps and sampled lager from a saucer the barman kept especially for him. He'd become an honorary member of the company and I was happy having him with me.

Being away from home for long periods was challenging for me as well as Jim but somehow we made it work. I never took for granted the difficulties my working life set for him or the steadfastness of his promise made all those years before to support me. The three months I had in Cheltenham made up the longest period I'd had yet of being unable to get home, even for a weekend, and I fretted over it. With my next job at Sheffield Crucible Theatre it was a relief to be back in the North and within commuting distance of home.

The Crucible is a lovely space to play that combines the virtues of a proscenium arch stage with a wide apron stage that thrusts deep out into the auditorium, giving it many of the features of theatre in the round. As well as entrances from the wings, entrances can be made from the voms, those tunnel-like entrances under the audience seating area. I was there to play the Hostess and the Widow in *The Taming of the Shrew*. The lovely director, Mark Brickman, decided Shakespeare's opening to the play, rarely done, in which the Hostess throws a drunken Christopher Sly out of the alehouse and he falls asleep and dreams up the play as we know it, needed sparking up. He charged us to go off and think up a new pre-play beginning and ending to the play, which finishes with Christopher Sly awakening from his dream on the alehouse steps.

The Sheffield Crucible of course hosts the national snooker competition so it didn't take long for Clive Kneller, who was playing Sly, and me to come up with the idea of a drunken snooker fan being cautioned for his loud behaviour by a Crucible staff barmaid. We honed some dialogue through improvisation and took it back to Mark who liked it but went one better. He said the argy-bargy should start in the theatre bar half an hour before curtain-up just as the audience were arriving. Then, around 7.30, when they were all seated in the auditorium and with the curtain about to go up, Clive could burst into the theatre shouting out he'd come for the snooker. I would be chasing after him to evict him. Cornered, he'd no choice but to run towards the stage followed by me, the house lights would go down, lights up on stage and we'd segue seamlessly into Shakespeare's lines.

After some initial false starts we had a whale of a time with me as a downtrodden Crucible Theatre barmaid in a blonde wig and a size 22 fat suit under a blouse and navy-blue skirt. Wearily I cleared glasses from the tables and answered questions from the audience about the time of the interval or where they could get change for the car park with, 'Don't ask me, love. I only work here. It's nearly the end of my shift and my feet are killing me,' while Clive propped up the bar getting steadily drunker and louder. When he did 'break into the auditorium', with me in pursuit going, 'Sir! Sir! You can't go in there. There's a play on. There *is* no snooker tonight', the audience looked away in embarrassment. As long as we kept our voices urgent but low key they took it for real and wanted to disassociate themselves. When we hit the stage they realised the joke had been against them and gave us a round of applause. There was also a credit in the programme which read '*The Taming of the Shrew*, by William Shakespeare, with additional material supplied by Clive Kneller and Vanessa Rosenthal'. We were proud of that.

My other part of the Widow near the end of the play involved an incredibly quick change from crimson wig and elaborate Elizabethan frock back into the fat suit to conclude the show. My dresser, Christine, had honed things to perfection until one Saturday night when I had gone to the theatre in my Laura Ashley size 10, navy pencil skirt. Christine came to the dressing room in the interval, as every night, to collect my hostess costume and have it waiting in the wings. Unfortunately, on this occasion, she picked up the wrong skirt. When I came off stage all went well at first. Wig off? Yes! Dress off? Yes! Fat suit on? Yes! Blouse on? Yes! And last the skirt? 'No! No!' I'm hissing out, 'That's my skirt.' 'Yes,' Christine hisses back, 'It's your skirt.' 'No,' I hiss again, 'It's *my* skirt. My own *me* skirt.' The full horror dawns on us. I can hear Clive wildly extemporising

Left:
Tom Stoppard
gains an Honorary
Doctorate from the
University of Leeds,
Jim in attendance as
Registrar, 1980.

In Łódź for the 40th
anniversary celebration of the
Technical University, 1985.

The military, 'medieval' Polish academic finery
and Jim, Łódź, 1985.

As the Jewish woman from the Warsaw ghetto
in Stuart Henson's *The Play of The Silver
Sword*, York Theatre Royal, 1984.

Contemplating the arch
leading to the area of the
former Łódź ghetto, 1985.

As Susan in
Mike Leigh's
Abigail's Party,
York Theatre Royal,
1985.

As Mrs Hardacre
in Walter Greenwood's
The Cure For Love,
York Theatre Royal,
1985.

As Mrs Darling in
J M Barrie's
Peter Pan,
York Theatre Royal,
1985.

Above: In my dressing room and as Fanny Margolies in Arthur Miller's
The American Clock, Newcastle Opera House, 1988.

Above left: Jim at Yale, 1991 and, right, me as Linda Loman in Miller's
Death Of A Salesman, Bolton Octagon, 1992.
Below left: As Mrs Birling in Priestley's *An Inspector Calls*, Bolton Octagon,
1992. Right: Jim on the night of his Honorary Doctorate dinner, Leeds, 1992.

With Jim at a wedding party in 1996.
Below left: Cast snap of Greenwood's *Love On
The Dole*, 1996. Right: Wetherby Road, 1998.

Williamson Park, Lancaster, as Miss Prism in
The Importance Of Being Earnest
and as The Duchess in *Alice in Wonderland*,
The Dukes Theatre, Lancaster, 1997.

Above left: As Mam in Alan
Bennett's *The Lady In The Van*,
Leeds Playhouse, 2002.

Above right: With Jim on
Chekhov's bench in Yalta, 2003.

Right: With Jim (post op.)
in Majorca, 2005.

As Marcia, with
Chris Wilkinson
as Maurice, in my
play *Modelling
Spitfires*,
New End
Theatre
Hampstead,
2010.

Top left: Adam and
Nerissa, with Bruno, Alec
and Sam at La Herradura,
2011.
Top right:
Emilia and Matt, with
Freddie and Robbie, 2006.
Left:
Freddie, Alec, Sam, Bruno
and Robbie, 2019.

First travels
with Nigel:
Chateau
Puivert
in Le Pays
de Cathares,
2010.

And now, left to right, and top to bottom: Monte Acuto, Scotland, Bialystok, Treblinka, Gubbio and home in a Marche palazzo, 2010 and on.

Above: With Lindesay Mace as the two
Karens in my play *Karen's Way*,
EIFF, 2012.   At left: As Irene Ruddock
in Bennett's *Lady of Letters*, and
below left, as Mrs Clegg in his *Enjoy*,
Leeds Playhouse, 2014.
Below: As Nina Hamnett in my play
Nina - Queen of Bohemia,
Galleries Tour, Spring, 2019.

some nonsense about Henry VIII as he marches up and down and waits for me. I've only two options: either I take off the fat suit and go on as a character who has shrunk to half her size in the space of two hours, or I brave it out half dressed. In any case there isn't time to take the fat suit off. I grab my own skirt in one hand, which only comes up to my knees (because the suit's a superb job with not only a fat torso but fat arms and knees and thighs), and in the other hand I yank the blouse down to cover as much of me as possible. Now I can't stand up straight; so I set off bunny-hopping up the vom to rescue Clive from his torture. As soon as the whole audience of 750 see me they start laughing. They are not exactly sure what it is that has gone wrong, but they know something looks very funny as a white blobby duvet, sprouting legs and arms hops forwards. Clive, like a trooper, makes mad goldfish eyes at me but keeps going. The rest of the cast, however, now assembled in the wings for the curtain call could be heard shrieking uncontrollably. They were still weeping unashamedly with laughter as we took our bows. Petruchio pushed me forwards with a big smile to take a solo bow and the whole audience roared its approval at its inclusion in the joke. We were united as one in the magic of theatre.

From the wide-thrust stage of The Crucible Theatre with all its possibilities, it seemed meant that I should return again to theatre in the round. I hadn't played in theatre in the round since my time at Scarborough and now I had another chance at Bolton Octagon Theatre and to stay in the North. I was there to do Mrs Birling in J B Priestley's *An Inspector Calls* and Linda Loman in Arthur Miller's *Death of a Salesman* and I relished it. Lawrence Till, the gifted director at the Octagon, had a wonderful understanding of theatre in the round and mounted an exciting production of *An Inspector Calls*. He brought the moral dilemma at the heart of the play to each member of the audience through skilful exploitation of the inherent intimacy of the auditorium. In theatre in the round there was no hiding away in a plush auditorium from the Inspector's interrogations. 'We are all responsible for each other,' the Inspector says as he relentlessly exposes each character's responsibility in the suicide of Eva Smith. The production had an edge and a strong visual focus in the set. At the beginning the self-satisfied Birling family are seated around a raised dining table, smug, assured and grand; by the end they have literally descended into the muck heaps of the street. Lawrence Till's production came a few years after the celebrated National Theatre production, which I didn't see until its revival years later, but I doubt it could have been as visceral in its effect.

Bolton, and then Sheffield again for another show, *The Good Sisters* by Michel Tremblay, were both reasonable commutes home on late night empty motorways. By 11.30 I was in my own kitchen able to talk through the day with Jim. These were stressful years for him and for all universities. The Thatcher cuts and efficiency drives, begun in the early eighties, meant staff cuts, which somehow had to be balanced alongside the government's insistence that universities needed to expand their intake numbers. 'How do we do that with less money and less staff?' Jim would say to me night after night.

For several weeks he was preoccupied with how to deal with it all. I would get back from Bolton to find him stretched out on the chesterfield in the dark. 'Why are you sitting in the dark doing nothing?' I'd ask. 'I am doing something,' he'd say, 'I'm thinking. Thinking is doing something.' Each university had already begun making its own objection to the cuts but nothing was happening in the way of a response. Weeks and months dragged on until Jim sat up from the chesterfield one night with a plan. 'Individually we're getting nowhere,' he told me, 'but if we put up a united response,

Government will have to listen to us.'

With renewed energy he decided to set up a secret meeting with his registrar colleagues from the other major non-Oxbridge universities. But where? Any part of London University had to be discounted on discretionary grounds. His secretary suggested various places which were dismissed before he settled on the Russell Hotel. Simple solutions were often the best. The Russell Hotel was where Jim always stayed when he was in London because it was handy for Kings Cross and the Senate House of London University. The first meeting was set up and was a success. It was followed by other equally successful meetings, at one of which Jim said they should give themselves a group name in their approaches to Government and idly, looking round his surroundings, suggested the 'Russell Group'. Eventually the vice-chancellors got wind of it all and felt threatened. Government, they felt, should be talking to the vice-chancellors, not to the registrars. Unceremoniously the registrars were ordered off the scene and the vice-chancellors took over, retaining not only the venue but the group name, which, by now had become established in Government circles as representing the major non-Oxbridge, civic universities. I knew none of this at the time. Jim never thought to mention any of it. He'd moved on to other knotty problems. It was left to Jim's secretary to fill me in many years later, not long before my eldest grandson Freddie was making applications to university in 2019 and telling me he was only interested in applying to universities that were within the Russell Group. He was duly surprised when I pointed out that the origins of the name had begun with his grandfather's liking for the Russell Hotel on his trips to London.

Chapter 8
RUTH

My mother had moved into the Morris Feinmann residential Jewish home against all opinion and advice from those who cared about her. Physically her osteoporosis had rapidly advanced to the point where walking any distance was no longer possible for her. For some while Judith had been living with her in the pleasant three-bedroom flat that had replaced the family home and helping out with the practical aspects of my mother's life alongside the demands of her post as senior lecturer in the English department at Manchester Metropolitan University. Now, to my delight, Judith had re-met her former husband, John Horsfield, and remarried him. Together they had a chance to build a new life that I hoped would bring them much happiness; unfortunately it left my mother living on her own.

I suggested a relocation to Leeds, which was vetoed, or a live-in companion, also vetoed. Then how about a housekeeper, Judith suggested, who could come in on a daily basis? None of these would do. Instead that May she removed herself temporarily into the Morris Feinmann home in order to 'try it out'. It was the very opposite of ideal. In the management's eyes, she'd basically taken herself there for extended respite care, with no commitment at that stage to full-time residency and so was allotted a basic single room that was not en suite. She had few of her pictures and objects from home about her in this temporary set-up. At night a commode was wheeled into her room; during the day she would make her way laboriously to the bathroom, pushing her Zimmer frame before her. It tore me in pieces to see this proud, stubborn, old woman, who had once run a large house, tastefully filled with the furniture and paintings she'd bought at country house auctions, reduced to such pathos. There was no need for any of it. This was gesture and protest against the unfairness of her new circumstances and I prayed she would soon accept some pragmatic solution and return to her flat.

Over the summer she had several longish breaks in Leeds when we went on outings to Ilkley and Harrogate and York, all places she enjoyed, but as the day came for her return to Manchester she would grow agitated. She had got it into her head that she was being whispered about behind her back and pointed out as a *shiksa*. I've no doubt a few of the elderly women in the home, formed by the attitudes of their Orthodox youth, did use the term unthinkingly which pained me for her. So, why was she going back there at all, scarecrow thin and worn out with worry when she had an alternative? Deep down I knew she had put herself there in rehearsal for a permanent residency in the future. I longed for her to end the experiment. With perseverance Judith and I would eventually find some solution in her flat that would suit her health-care needs. Sadly events overtook us. By September her breathlessness, caused by a deterioration in her heart condition, meant the home advised me she wasn't fit to make any journeys and moved her into the nursing wing. Barely four months after she had moved in, she died of a massive stroke and was buried next to my father with verses from the Book of Ruth recited at her grave at her request.

'Entreat me not to leave thee, or return from following after thee; for whither thou goest, I will go, and there will be my lodging; thy people shall be my people and thy God my God. Where thou diest will I die and there will I be buried; the Lord do so unto me also, if aught but death part thee and me.'

I felt the pity and pain of it like a physical punch that plunged me into depression.

My mother's married life was lived out in the Jewish community, which in her eyes, and mine, constantly held her up for examination. With her fierce pride she had planned a good death in a Jewish residential home as proof of her commitment to her adopted faith. The early rejections she had experienced had left damage to the gentle, unconfident side of her nature. There have been many robust Jewish men and women who have married non-Jewish partners and gone on to live entirely happy, secular lives outside the community. Even within the community times have changed a lot and a non-Jewish partner is welcomed in more genuinely than my mother ever experienced, certainly in Reform Judaism. I see no evidence of the children of such marriages feeling outsiders but then there is no forum for truly honest discussion on the subject. The non-Jewish partner is frequently referred to as a 'convert', not in any judgemental sense but simply as a matter of identification. Or is it truly non-judgemental, persisting as it does even after fifty or sixty years? Why does it matter? Is this a throw-back to some atavistic instinct to preserve a pure gene pool? Words like 'tribal' and 'racist' are outlawed in our politically correct world but sweeping them under the carpet paralyses genuine discussion from both points of view. I am proud to identify myself as Jewish but always the worm in my head, like some Faustian imp, jumps in and says, as Paul said all those years ago, 'Who are you kidding? According to Orthodox Jewish teaching a Jew is someone born of a Jewish mother and you, Vanessa, are actually a hybrid.'

I struggled through a dark period after her death. Alongside the anger I felt at the injustice of the treatment she'd received from my father's family and others, I discovered in myself a deep-seated resentment of her.

Because of her I couldn't claim unbroken Jewish descent. On the one hand I was mourning a beloved parent and on the other I was attaching blame to her, not to my father, which was unfair. This painful conflict of emotions took me briefly into counselling but I was an old hand at my own problems and wearied of trying to explain myself. Slowly I saw more clearly that being bound to her silence on the subject of her non-Jewish family and upbringing was harmful and dishonest. I needed to be bold where she had been unable to be and chance was to be on my side.

I was working again at the BBC in Radio Drama, Manchester, when a close actor friend congratulated me on a novel of mine that had been shortlisted for a significant prize for first-time novelists. Our conversation in the green room was overheard by the director as she flitted between studio and green room. 'I didn't know you wrote, Vanessa!' she said. 'A novel. Not plays,' I said. 'I don't write plays.' And it was true. I had always written poems, diaries, novels but never drama. 'Oh what nonsense,' she said. 'Of course you can write plays. You're an actor for goodness sake. Go away and write me a play.'

So, I did. I went home and began to write a play about the thing that occupied me most: my parents' mixed marriage and it was as if confronting this central issue in my life was a release from something that had been holding back my writing for a long time. My mother's death had freed me. Concealment had been part of the contents in our locked family cupboard. Don't tell. Don't talk about things and here was I chucking everything out into the open air to let in some light and it felt right. From then on I began a dual career as playwright and actor.

That first play, about my parents, for BBC Radio 4 was called *Jerusalem North West* and is set in Manchester. Its last scene takes place in a Jewish residential home where Maggie (Hilda) is dying and hearing Harry (Leonard) in her head, as she has done throughout the play.

HARRY   Funny...I never thought I'd find you here.

MAGGIE   Where else did you think I'd be?

HARRY   You wouldn't catch me dying in a Jewish residential home.

MAGGIE   You wouldn't need to to establish bona fides.

HARRY   Is that why you did it?

MAGGIE   I did it to be near you.

HARRY   I know that, Maggie. You're a better Jew than me.

MAGGIE   I loved you, Harry. The rest just flowed as a consequence.

HARRY   I gave up very little. Was it too high a price to pay?

(BEATS)

MAGGIE   No, dear. It wasn't.

HARRY   What about the things *you* gave up?

MAGGIE   I never think about them.

HARRY   You sure? I couldn't bear it if you've lived with regret all these years.

MAGGIE   Sssh. I'm sure. Perfectly sure.

HARRY   We made the disease between us and then we were each other's remedy.

MAGGIE   Ourselves against the world. Yes. (FIERCELY) *I did love you Harry. It's just I'm so alone now.*

HARRY   What do you mean, alone? I'm here. Have I ever let you down?

MAGGIE   I was an only child. I'd no family of my own.

HARRY   You've always been so strong.

MAGGIE   And I am. Hold my hand, dear.

HARRY   I'm holding it.

MAGGIE   That's good.

HARRY   I never looked at another woman all these years.

MAGGIE   I know that.

HARRY   So close your eyes now. (PAUSE) Good-night, sweet Maggie Rapunzel, Daughter of Israel.

The play closes here as Maggie recites softly those same lines from the Book of Ruth that she has chosen and lived towards even as the music of 'I Know That My Redeemer Liveth' swells up in her head from her childhood and then all of it is drowned out as Harry starts to recite the *kaddish* prayer for the dead.

> *Yis'ga'dal v'yis'kadash sh'may ra'bbo, b'olmo dee'vro chir'usay v'yamlich malchu'say, b'chayaychon uv'yomay'chon uv'chayay d'chol bais Yisroel.*

Writing the play was cathartic and painful; also honest. Two years after battling with it all I made a conscious decision to join the Reform synagogue in Leeds knowing I belonged there more than anywhere else, although I still lacked confidence in my entitlement. My first steps were infrequent and tentative. I knew no one, and while I knew a wide circle of people in the city after twenty-five years of living there, I knew no one there and felt inhibited from explaining myself or explaining my absence for so long. I had arrived fully-formed so to speak, a long-married wife and mother with nothing to show of all that life except myself. But there was much comfort in the familiarity of the services and in quietly standing at the back and taking it all in. Ironically I knew my mother would have been delighted if she could have seen me there. This was what she had always wished for me.

Chapter 9
NEW HORIZONS

I had reached middle age and as well as returning to my Jewish roots, life events were crowding in thick and fast. At sixty-three Jim had decided to retire. The crisis in university funding had led, with the gradual inevitability which Jim had foreseen for several years, to the concept of a modern university that would look increasingly towards a business model for its future. It was no longer the world Jim knew and enjoyed of great research institutions built on traditions of scholarship. A mixture of boredom when faced with more cuts (been there, done that) and stress when faced with further clamours for expansion, expansion, expansion had brought him to this point. A new vice-chancellor had recently been appointed, heralding in a new era and the timing seemed apt. That summer he was awarded an honorary doctorate and we had a happy day of celebration that was far from signalling an ending but rather an underlining of new directions with a bigger event to follow a month later in the shape of Nerissa's wedding.

She had been in New York for three years by this time, laying down the foundations for what was to become an impressive career in high-end advertising, working out of an advertising agency on the seventy-ninth floor of the Empire State Building. There she had met Karl, a Dubliner, who was working for NatWest bank as a futures trader. In the impossibly romantic setting of Battery Park in Manhattan, events had moved fast. Sadly this young marriage wasn't to last, but the wedding day itself was a joyous celebration of our family life and of how far we'd all travelled together. The following day we had another party in the garden for fifty guests. This was never intended to be so great a number but somehow had snowballed. Over twenty of the guests had flown from New York for the wedding and a dozen more had come from Ireland. Jim and I had wanted to offer some hospitality at home. The weeks before had seen me cooking four whole salmon for the freezer along with half a dozen large gateaux. Jim had ordered garden tables and fold-up chairs and booked taxis to ferry the guests from the country house hotel where they were staying. It was madness, like having two wedding days back-to-back. Exhaustion hit us like a sledge hammer; we couldn't even face the clearing up for thirty-six hours. If this was supposed to be Jim's retirement it was going like a whirlwind. We were also just about to complete on a pied-à-terre we'd bought in Chiswick in a thirties block next to Queen Charlotte's Hospital with a moving-in date set for a few weeks later.

West London was a good base with Emilia round the corner in a house share with other young professionals at the start of her career in the Civil Service. From Stamford Bridge tube station Jim had easy access to the Public Record Office in Kew for the archives he sought in relation to the work he'd started on technical higher education in Britain. He'd long held a view that nineteenth-century Britain's failure to follow up her industrial lead had put her far behind her European comparators for decades. In Jim's opinion Oxford and Cambridge's 800-year-old tradition of largely educating only clerics and administrators, 'because gentlemen didn't dirty their hands with engineering and the like', had held the country back. Shades of the old Marxist lived on. Now, with a Nuffield grant, he would get down to publishing several papers over the next few years, examining the foundation of technical universities in the early twentieth century, as Britain finally awoke to the urgent need. The industrial towns in the North of England, where most of the country's wealth was to be found, had known for some time they were technologically lagging behind France and the Netherlands. With trips planned to Delft and Paris in the pipeline, Jim had a full timetable planned.

But before any of this had properly begun, he tagged himself on to the tour I was engaged in that autumn with The Actor's Touring Company in remotest West Wales. The outgoing director of The ATC, a Welshman, had wanted, as his swansong, to do the first English language production of the *Mabinogion*, and after opening in Cardiff, we were touring all over Wales. Jim turned up frequently like a latter-day stage-door-Johnny, enjoying the camaraderie of our troupe of wandering players. He cheerfully accepted the snatched meals in odd cafés and fish bars and offered to write a piece for the *Times Higher Educational Supplement* on the comparative value of fish and chips in half a dozen Welsh towns but it was turned down by the then editor on the grounds of it being 'too frivolous' for a recent Emeritus Registrar. No sense of humour, was Jim's comment.

In Carmarthen, on a bitterly cold night, a drama student friend of Hugh's, the actor playing the Warrior, turned up to help us with the get out. Dressed in a fawn duffle coat and still suffering badly from acne, he was very pleasant and friendly with striking light blue eyes. He and Hugh had grown up together in Swansea and were trying to get their own theatre company off the ground. Later, when the show finally landed at Sadlers Wells, he turned up again in an Islington pub on election night and greeted us all like old friends. As he was leaving, Hugh turned to me and said 'Mike still has two more terms to do at RADA but when he leaves he'll be a star. Just you wait. He's phenomenal.' 'What's his other name then?' I asked. 'He's Michael Sheen,' Hugh said. He was right about 'phenomenal'.

By now Jim had decided that being in the thick of a theatre crowd was the perfect balance between life in the archives of the PRO (Public Records Office) and life on the road. I'd written a play about the poet Edward Thomas and his wife Helen, based on his poems, and her painfully honest account of their married life. Jim decided to come too when we took it to the Edinburgh Fringe Festival that year. As well as me playing Helen, and an actor playing Edward Thomas, the story of their lives was told through interludes of music, aptly chosen and superbly performed by David Riley, the violinist from the orchestra of Opera North, and Marion Raper, a highly regarded piano accompanist.

I had been to the Festival years before as a student, but now it had morphed out of all recognition and the fight to secure an audience against all the competing shows on offer at the same time was high. We deputed Jim to go and stand on the Royal Mile and hand out leaflets. It was a role he took to with enthusiasm, standing on the North Bridge in his beloved Boston Red Sox baseball cap worn back to front; he bought it when he'd attended a course at Harvard and now it was inseparable from him. Fully in the spirit of things, he quickly became adept at tearing down the publicity posters of others and putting up our own with the Blu Tack he kept in his jacket pocket, while talking to all and everyone at length. The result was that at our opening show (it had previously opened at York Theatre Royal where Jim had seen it) he was nowhere to be found. When he did bowl up he said he'd got talking to two lively young girls who made him promise he'd go to their show that afternoon instead of ours. I think they were not only lively but very easy on the eye, though he probably saw more of them than he intended. The piece apparently had a high erotic content and as there were only four of them in the audience he felt honour bound to show his appreciation. After that there were endless jokes at Jim's expense along the lines that he'd turned down high culture for something more titillating.

I might have laughed less if I'd known that the show I'd be doing only a few years later in the Studio at the Royal Exchange Theatre, Manchester, entailed a scene in the buff. Called *Still Time*, this wonderfully tender chamber piece for four actors by Stephanie McKnight had a scene in the second act set on a naturist beach, where four middle-aged friends are having a day out. I'd said at the audition I'd no qualms about the nudity because no one would be expecting to see the body beautiful with middle-aged actors on view but when I found out the show was to be peripatetic with the audience walking from scene to scene and standing throughout, a slight panic set in. To make matters worse we didn't appear nude but strolled through the audience at the start of the scene in shorts and T-shirts until we 'found' a grassy knoll where we could undress to 'have a swim'; or as the *Independent* put it 'a grassy knoll where the brave cast could strip off'. At the end of the scene it went to a blackout in which we each grabbed our own clothes and left the acting area as quickly as possible. I still had my eyesight problems in going from light into dark or vice versa which went way back to Farnham days. It was all I could do to grab a bundle of clothes and get myself off. There was no end of high jinks behind the flat with my urgent whispers of 'I've picked up the wrong knickers, again!'

But all of this was as nothing compared to Emilia bringing her serious boyfriend Matt (later to be her husband) to see the show. I doubt many other mothers-in-law can trump this as, if not the first meeting, then only the second meeting with a future son-in-law. Of course I'd warned her where to stand to see as little of me as possible but for some reason the pair of them decided to plonk themselves down on the floor in a corner and as the action moved towards them, they got a wonderful view from the ground level up. Suffice it to say that on that occasion I found a hundred and one ways to drape a bath towel.

Having the Chiswick base was a new dimension in our lives. For the first time in years I was in rehearsal in London and returning each evening to my own London pad. It felt different; it was different. I imagined what my whole career might have been like if I'd been London-based throughout. I cannot believe it would have been more fulfilling, maybe more successful in terms of opportunities; maybe more rewarding, but by now I was a declared Northerner through and through and proud of it. I had lived in London and the South for less than five years, which made me a country cousin who enjoyed frequent visiting rights. At the time of my marriage it was still rare for actors to live outside London, but by now every large city had its cohort of actors with many of them involved in setting up actors co-operative agencies where they found the work for each other using the commission money to finance office rental space and utilities. Some of these, very much a feature of the 1980s, were highly successful and had begun to be well regarded professionally. Manchester, Leeds, Birmingham, Newcastle, Oxford and Brighton all had enough Equity members living locally to hold their own meetings. Granada Television in Manchester and Yorkshire Television in Leeds offered more work while the BBC Broadcast Studios in Manchester favoured Northern-based actors because they were cheaper, not requiring accommodation expenses.

It was a curious reversal therefore to find myself in London rehearsing a quintessentially Northern play, *Love on the Dole*, by

Walter Greenwood. Not only was it a Northern play but one that had a particular personal connection to me.

In 1934 my mother was working occasionally at the Manchester Repertory Theatre as a professional actress while she qualified at the Northern College of Music as an elocution teacher: practices that were fairly common at the time. Twenty-four years old, tall, slim and a striking redhead from Rochdale, Walter Greenwood was very taken with her and wanted her for the lead role of Sally Hardcastle in *Love on the Dole*. Things went quite a way down the line, in terms of readings and early rehearsals, before my father issued an ultimatum. She must choose between the play and London or their prospective marriage. Things were already fraught enough for them at this point with my mother's conversion in process and the disapproval of both families at its height, and she unhesitatingly chose the marriage. After that, in her own words, 'the part went to an unknown ASM called Wendy Hiller'[2], and the rest, as they say, is history. For years I'd known this story, which my mother told with no sense of regret, but it made a nice puff in terms of marketing the show to the press in the various towns on the tour schedule. Here was I playing Mrs Hardcastle, being mother to my mother so to speak in a neat reversal.

Something about acting in a classic Lancashire play so soon after my mother's death stirred up more grief for me. For the first time I was curious about her family. I wanted more than the few bits and pieces I'd been given as hearsay and set about playing detective. I knew that my maternal great-great-grandfather James Whittam, a well-respected auctioneer and farmer in Rochdale, had owned a terrace of

---

2   Regarded as one of Britain's great dramatic talents, she was made an Officer of the Order of the British Empire (OBE) in 1971 and raised to Dame Commander (DBE) in 1975. In 1984 she was awarded an honorary doctorate from the University of Manchester. Source: Wikipedia

houses for rent in the town. These houses had eventually been sold but not the land they were built on, which yielded a peppercorn ground rent each year administered from a family trust inherited by his great-grandchildren. Every Christmas there was a card from my mother's first cousin John Brierley, with a cheque for her annual share. His father and my maternal grandmother were brother and sister, and so I'd always known of him but never met him. His address was in my mother's padded address book that used to live in a drawer of the Welsh dresser in the hall, so finding it hardly amounted to taxing detective work on my part but my letter, coming to him from out of the blue, must have struck him as deeply suspicious. In fact he told me so when he and his wife invited Jim and me for tea. 'What was I after?' he asked me in blunt Lancashire manner.

John Brierley was an impressive looking man in his early seventies, father of three and grandfather of seven. He'd recently retired from a directorship in the textile industry and lived in a pretty Georgian house on the edge of Bolton. From him I learned he was one of four brothers, all Lancashire farmers. It was very curious to discover, in my fifties, that I had vast numbers of second and third cousins I'd only ever guessed at, many of them called Whittam or Zachary in some combination of old family names. Once again I questioned my parents' wisdom in the relegation of the Lancashire family to offstage roles. It was done to bring up me and my sister within a single Jewish cultural influence but layers of family secrets drag in words like shame and denial. I felt cheated; no one had consulted me and now it all felt immeasurably too late. I didn't blame John Brierley for his question. The only answer I could give him was the honest one: I'd wanted to reach out and find out more of where I'd come from on my mother's side, a task which John's wife Joyce threw herself into enthusiastically.

From a sideboard she produced a wealth of family papers and

newspaper cuttings to flesh out the little I knew; family genealogy was a hobby of hers she explained. My maternal grandmother Ellen and John's father Arthur were brought up in Rochdale, where their father Kershaw owned a butcher's shop, supplied with meat from his own farm near Bury. Kershaw died young and unusually, in circumstances that seemed to characterise the kind of man he was. An early member of the Primrose League founded 'to uphold and support God, Queen and country', he was one of a long line of staunch Lancashire patriots but the only one I knew of whose death was indirectly attributable to his politics. In the bank in Rochdale around 1902, he met some soldiers returning from the Boer War and insisted on taking them out for a slap-up lunch to congratulate them on serving their country, saying he could do no less. Unfortunately, one of them was a carrier for the typhus then rife in the Transvaal and Kershaw contracted the infection and died from it. The story appeared in the local press, attracting letters of approval and condolence.

That afternoon, courtesy of Joyce, I found out a lot more. Here was enough material to furnish several more plays. The more I heard the more I felt proud of these Lancashire roots. Two Brierley great-uncles, James and Zachary, built the Winter Gardens in Llandudno with a family fortune that came from Creams Coach Company, which made charabancs. During the war, under Zachary's son, also named Zachary, the company was turned over to making tanks and Zachary Brierley was knighted for his services to the war effort. There were a few skeletons too. Tales of disinheritance for real or perceived transgressions, quarrels over land and family feuds over goods and chattels that ended up with the wrong son or daughter-in-law. I came away with a more solid understanding of what had gone before me but it was half of the story of who I was. The time had come to make that return journey to Poland and find out about the rest.

Chapter 10
BIALYSTOK TO BURNLEY

We flew first to Cracow and walked its medieval streets and were awed by the evidence of a once vibrant, large Jewish community stretching back hundreds of years. Perhaps this lesson in scale was the right preparation for our memorial visit to Auschwitz. There are so few words that have not been written and read already. This was late autumn and the vast *appelplatz* looked cold and empty. It was impossible to imagine its prisoners in a sub-zero Polish winter, standing for hours on end for roll-call, clad in what amounted to no more than striped pyjamas; or to think of them in their huts, stacked three tiers high to sleep six to a platform like bundles of warehouse goods. The murder of so many was horrific but the details of the depravity meted out to all before their ending in a gas chamber overwhelmed the soul. Returning to the beauty of Cracow's main square, sitting at a café table looking out on the magnificent Renaissance Cloth Hall felt dishonourable. I wanted to leave the city. We visited the Kupa synagogue so I could say *kaddish* and then I was glad to make our way to the station.

Getting to Bialystok put us very much on our own. No tourist map included this textile city in the North East of the country. First we took the train to Warsaw Central and then transferred to Warsaw East to start a journey in which the station names in Cyrillic script were incomprehensible to us. For a while we sat in silence while vast forests of silver birch trees sped by. Eventually, with the help of fellow passengers and some attempts of mine at pronunciation, we arrived in the right place and as I climbed down from the train I was overwhelmed with emotion. Only one generation separated me from my grandfather, who would have stood on this very platform to start his journey westwards. The beautiful Russian Byzantine façade of the station that I now looked at on my arrival was the same façade he saw as he left as a seventeen-year-old boy. Several months previously I'd found his naturalisation papers in the Public Records Office that stated: 'I swear that I am a subject of Russia having been born in Bialystok in Grodno, the son of Jacob and Leah Rosenthal.' He had signed it with his name, the first physical evidence I had of a grandfather who died twenty years before I was born. I was moved to tears as I read it in that public space and now I was here to walk the streets he grew up in. I'd like to think he knew.

Before the war the Jewish population of the city of Bialystok was 39 000 with over a hundred synagogues, Jewish hospitals, schools, libraries, theatres, newspapers. Its inhabitants spoke Yiddish, Byelorussian, Russian, Polish and German in a thriving cosmopolitan community. There was little evidence of it left. In the Jewish cemetery the headstones had been deliberately desecrated and smashed. In an act of gross humiliation, Jews were ordered by the Nazis to collect pieces of the stone to repair the roads. Here and there in the old town Hebrew letters appeared amongst the cobble stones with the name of someone's mother, father or child engraved on them. A plaque at 79, Sienkiewicza Street, marked the Jewish gymnasium where my grandfather would have gone to school. Another plaque, out in the silver birch forests surrounding the town, marked the spot where thousands of men, women and children had perished. Forced at gunpoint to march out of the town and strip naked under the trees, they were then ordered to line up at the edge of a trench they had previously dug themselves before being mown down into the mass grave. Two hundred thousand from the ghetto and from the surrounding regions were murdered in Treblinka and on 27 June 1941, the so-called Red Friday, 800 more men were pistol-butted into the Great Synagogue by a large motorised German unit, who drank a toast to death before barricading the whole building against escape and setting it alight. Somewhere amongst all that number were remnants of my grandfather's extended family; of *my* family; of Jacob and Leah, and all the descendants of their brothers and sisters and cousins.

I had come in search of one of them specifically called Hershel Rozental. My father had spoken of him a few times as a relative. How he knew about him I never asked when I could have done (a familiar story to many people) nor did I know which branch of the family he was descended from. On the subject of the Holocaust my father's feelings were too deeply felt to allow much conversation. I believe he felt a generic survivor's guilt. The counterpart of his generation of Jews across Europe had largely perished. Speaking at all of Poland reminded him that only his father's emigration rescued him from the persecution. The tone of his voice changed and his words became sparse and reluctantly given up. It created an atmosphere in which my questions would be unwelcome and I rarely tested it. The only anecdote he ever told me, again related in few words, referred to his father's childhood in the inn his parents kept. As a small boy his father was asleep by the fire when Prussian soldiers came into the inn and seeing a little 'yid' curled up in the hearth thought it fun to take up the poker and brand his face. Someone must have intervened before there was more serious injury inflicted but all his life, my father said, Eleazer bore the scar.

So, altogether, I had very little to go on in tracing Hershel Rozental. All I knew was that, at the time of the German occupation, he was a young student at Warsaw University who later played some brave part in the Bialystok ghetto uprising. Until I started looking, prior to this visit I had even been ignorant of the fact that the Bialystok ghetto uprising was second in importance only to the Warsaw ghetto uprising. Now with the internet, a lot more information was available. As I started searching, I was astonished to see Hershel Rozental's name come up several times, including a cross reference to the *Jewish Encyclopaedia*. It was from this source I learned that Hershel was a prominent activist in Dror, a Zionist youth group, who had fled to the forests with other partisans as soon as the German occupation began. When word reached him in August 1943 of the Nazi intention to liquidate those that remained in the ghetto, he came back from the forests to join in a general discussion about what to do. Ephraim Barash, the ghetto leader, argued for compliance with the Nazi edicts as a way of saving as many lives as possible but Hershel Rozental, along with Mordecai Tenenbaum, a fellow Zionist, argued for armed resistance. The impassioned case Hershel put forward somehow survived and here was I reading his speech on my computer in the comfort of my living room in Leeds, nearly sixty years later.

'Here in Bialystok we are fated to live out the last act of this blood-stained tragedy. What can we do and what should we do? The way I see it the situation really is that the great majority in the ghetto and of our group are sentenced to die. Our fate is sealed. We have never looked on the forest as a place in which to hide, we have looked on it as a base for battle and vengeance. But the tens of young people who are going into the forests now do not seek a battlefield there, most of them will lead beggars' lives there and most likely will find a beggar's death. In our present situation our fate will be the same, beggars all. There is only one thing left for us, therefore, and it is: organizing a collective act of resistance in the ghetto at any cost, to consider the ghetto to be our "Musa Dagh" (a mountain in Turkey and the scene of a successful resistance to the Armenian Genocide) and to add a chapter of honor to Jewish Bialystok and to our movement.'

– Hershel Rozental.

I found the words incredibly moving and felt proud to have some connection to the bravery of a man like Hershel Rozental, who had inevitably perished in the uprising. Working out my exact connection to him I quickly realised was a tall order. I didn't know his date of birth or exactly where he'd been born. Without these the only way was to get back to my grandparents' records and construct a line of descent that might eventually turn up his name. Practical obstacles, not least my lack of Polish, defeated me on such a short trip.

Only with the advances in the transposition of many records on to microfiche over the next dozen years was there a better chance of finding out more. I planned my second trip fifteen years later with the intention of searching for my grandparents' records in the city's records office. These I hoped would take me to my great-grandparents' generation that might provide the start of a family tree. But, though I had someone with me who spoke good English, she didn't speak Russian in which most of the nineteenth-century records were written as part of the Russian Empire. With much difficulty and the help of a Russian–Polish dictionary we found my grandfather's birth certificate, giving details of my great-grandparents and their address in the town, nothing else. Beyond that, only time and a professional genealogist could solve the rest. The young archivist, who was there to help, apologised for having no Russian either. I looked at him and judged him to be in his mid-twenties, making him born around 1990. Of course he didn't speak Russian. Post the collapse of the Berlin Wall, Russian was no longer the second language in schools, for obvious reasons. I thanked him for his time and accepted my defeat as part of the accelerated rate of change in Poland. Between my trip to Lodz in 1985 and my first trip to Bialystok in 2000 there were marked changes, but this trip in 2015 was of another order altogether. Clean, wide, well-lit streets with shopping malls and food halls gave way to landscaped open spaces with water features. Designer shops and mobile phone shops were everywhere and in a delicatessen café the coffee machines hissed away. I wasn't sure that I would ever come again. My Bialystok was a place of imagined shadows and imagined people, 39 000 of them, including Hershel Rozental but on my return from my first trip I wrote a play about some of them.

Exchanges in Bialystok, while foregrounding the terrible Holocaust years, deals with a personal reconciliation with the past, when Professor Goldber, a criminal rights lawyer, finally revisits his father's birth city for the first time. There he finds himself in collision with a retired librarian, Miss Harris, who has come on a similar mission, only in her case to find out about a father, Samuel Harris, who was a pastor in the Barbican Mission in Bialystok.

The Barbican Mission were an evangelical church made up of Hebrew Christians, Jewish men and women, operating extensively in Poland in the mid-twentieth century, who sincerely believed that

God had already sent his Jewish Messiah to live and die amongst them and who sought to convert other Jews to their faith.

To many they were anathema and viewed with repugnance, but in the cemetery in Bialystok I had discovered the grave of a Jewish man, born in Hackney in the East End of London, who had died of typhus in the ghetto in 1942. I was very curious to learn that he was an ordained minister of the Barbican Mission. How did he come to be buried in a Jewish cemetery? As I pieced together more of the story, through the help of the present-day Barbican Mission in Tunbridge Wells, I was profoundly moved.

Samuel Harris had taken himself voluntarily to live in the ghetto because he felt compelled to help the community, even though his British nationality and his calling might have saved him. In a speech in the play, taken from his diary (a diary that exists in the Barbican Mission's archives), he explains himself.

'The fate of the Jews is pitiable and we have abandoned all the Mission's work to do what we can to help. What drugs were in the dispensary we have brought with us and give out freely. There is widespread disease everywhere. The early severe winter is an added scourge to the many afflictions suffered by the Jews. A distribution of warm clothing is under way but there is not enough for the need and we must do more, much more if we are to make any real difference.'

On his death from typhoid, the community in the ghetto put aside all personal prejudice against a man who was born a Jew but embraced Christianity, and at great material sacrifice to themselves, for by then they had nothing, organised a Jewish burial for him. They wanted to honour his Jewish identity and family but most importantly to pay tribute to him as a righteous man. This little-known story of humanity had taken place within the ghetto while, in the Nazi world outside the ghetto, hatred and racial persecution advanced its madness. There could not have been a greater contrast or a sharper plea for compassion and I hoped it might make the case for universal tolerance. Eventually the play was chosen to represent the BBC at the European Script Broadcasting Union Award in Helsinki, after which I hoped it might have an even further reach.

The play was produced and directed brilliantly and memorably by David Ian Neville with the wonderful actor, David Horovitch, playing Professor Goldber, in a nuanced and sensitive performance with steel at its core. He had been at Central when I was there and I had always admired his work. The comic genius, David Schneider, played the roguish Polish guide, Dariusz Pogonowski. David had a doctorate in Yiddish drama and during the days of the recording entertained and enlightened us all in the green room with his fluency in Yiddish. I only have a vocabulary of odd words but David has an entire language. Yiddish is such a vigorous language, even without precise understanding, you catch the drift from the sound of words alone. Words like *chutzpah*, *nosh*, *schlep*, *schmooze* and *shtick* speak for themselves. As is often the case a sombre play was relieved by much offstage hilarity.

Autumn had prematurely leapt towards winter by the time we reached home after Poland. It was a cold day with rain when we set out on a research trip to Worsthorne Moor above Burnley, in connection with something I was writing based on a family ghost story that I'd known for a long time but only recently placed geographically after a visit to Burnley Local History Library. Now armed with an Ordnance Survey map and strong shoes we set out to walk the walk of the exact location.

In 1840 Cant Clough farm, high up on the moor and marked to

this day on the map, was owned by a Whittam ancestor named Robert Whittam, a brother or cousin of my great-great-grandfather James Whittam. By all accounts Robert Whittam was a crusty, autocratic farmer who turned inwards after his wife died, shortly after giving birth to a daughter, another Ellen, leaving Robert Whittam to bring her up, together with her brother John. Thrown together, brother and sister were very close. At twenty Ellen was disinherited for marrying Robert Whittam's farmhand, Arnold Clayton, and banished from Cant Clough. It was then the couple decided to emigrate to Australia leaving John heartbroken. He believed that he would never see his sister again but she promised to return before she died, and so she did but not in earthly form!

THE DROVER'S PATH

The wind howls round a moorland farmhouse in the Pennines.
Very distant noises of sheep off. The farm kitchen. A November evening,
1850. A new born baby cries off. A woman sshs the baby.

WOMAN (OFF)   Sssh. Sssh. There, you've done very well, Mrs Whittam and such a bonny baby, such a beauty.

ROB (WRITING)   Ellen Mary Whittam. Born the twentieth of November 1850. Cant Clough Farm, Worsthorne. Entered into the family bible by her father, Robert Whittam. (HE STOPS WRITING) On a raw night at the top of the world. Only the kestrel and the fox up here for company, lass, and the wind howling round our chimney.

A door creeps open a few inches.

ROB   Yes, you can come on in now, John William. Come in and see what we've got for you in the next room. A bonny sister. You'll like that now, won't you? A playmate of your own. Mind you look out for her and take good care of her. Will you do that for me?

A ghostly montage of hide and seek. Young John calls and calls over a wide distance. Young Ellen answers from far off. The sound of her giggles and laughter loop over and over John's speeches.

YOUNG JOHN   (FRANTIC) Ellen! Ellen! Ellen! Where are you?
YOUNG ELLEN   (GIGGLING) Over here.
YOUNG JOHN   Where?
YOUNG ELLEN   Here!
YOUNG JOHN   But I can't see you.
YOUNG ELLEN   I'm *here!* Where I always am. Come and find me!

The words 'find me' and the laughter echo on and on and we hear a folk song sung softly.

> One man shall mow my meadow
> Two men shall gather it together
> Two men and one more
> Shall shear my lambs and ewes and rams
> And gather my gold together

From the visitors' car park we set off in the rain up the steep track to find the farmhouse. As we climbed higher the clouds turned blacker and the wind got up, flipping the map I was holding backwards and forwards. Near the top of the path we rounded a corner and were suddenly exposed to the full force of the wind on what was now open moorland and it was bitterly cold. Although the track had been renovated to provide access for ramblers and mountain bikers, only the brave, or the foolish, would have ventured out on such a day. As the crow flew we were about twenty miles across the moor to Wuthering Heights. In front of us suddenly was a great expanse of water easily identifiable on the map as Cant Clough Reservoir. 'But where's the farm?' I shouted above the wind. 'I don't know,' Jim shouted back. We looked all round and could see nothing only the gable outline of a building on a path below us that led back down again from the top. 'That must be it,' I said. 'Not big enough,' Jim said. 'That's more like a barn.' We tramped around some more without success with the wind moaning about us and then it started to hail. Great vicious stones of it that stung our faces. It was not weather to linger out in for long. 'We need to get back,' Jim shouted and started off down the other track. As we came closer to the building we'd seen from above, it was clear it was a handsome brick barn with a timber roof. 'That's old,' Jim said. 'Looks late eighteenth century.' Next to it was a modern, rather ugly-looking bungalow, dwarfed in size by the magnificent barn. I approached the front of it and stopped in my tracks. There on the front gate was the name, Cant Clough Farm. I gawped at it in disappointment. 'That can't be it,' I said. 'Something is wrong with this map.' But by now we had attracted some attention and a man in work clothes came down the path towards us to ask if we were lost. I pointed to the map and told him what we were looking for and why. He smiled shyly and nodded his head. He was the shepherd who rented the present-day Cant Clough farm he explained. He had a widespread flock on Shedden Moor that he reached by quad bike. Soon he'd be bringing them down to winter over on the lower ground of Four Day field that stood in front of us. 'An old name?' Jim asked. 'Oh, yes. It was called that because it used to take four men from the farm four days to mow the hay back then.' Did he know then what happened to the original Cant Clough Farm? I asked. He smiled. 'It's under the reservoir,' he said. 'There was a compulsory purchase order in 1861 when the reservoir was built. Must have been very near here because this barn belonged to it.' I stared and stared at the barn and felt goosebumps. So much of the story belonged in that barn. Its bricks and mortar had been witness to sad events. Jim must have felt it too because after we left the shepherd, he turned back up the path again and I followed. For several minutes we stood and watched the wind whipping up the surface of the water of the reservoir. Did I imagine I saw the top of a chimney stack of the buried Whittam farm? Who was there to watch as the water flooded into its kitchen and parlour? And what of the lives that lived out their days under its roof? Jim shook his head in disbelief. 'In one autumn,' he said, 'we've travelled from Eastern Poland to this and you're directly connected with both places.' His remark seemed to sum up neatly my own ambiguity about my roots.

Chapter 11

NORMANDY AND BEYOND

We celebrated the coming of the Millennium in Honfleur; my idea. Shakespeare had something to do with it too. I wanted to take the whole family somewhere redolent of quintessential English history, of success and triumph. What more authentic place than the vasty fields of Northern France, for ever associated with Shakespeare's play *Henry V* and the Battle of Agincourt. Jim was enthusiastic; also characteristically relieved to have me take over the organisation of the trip which left him free to reminisce. He often talked about Laurence Olivier's film *Henry V* that had come out in 1944 and used to quote great chunks of it around Remembrance Day.

> 'For he to-day that sheds his blood with me
> Shall be my brother; be he ne'er so vile,
> This day shall gentle his condition:
> And gentlemen in England now a-bed
> Shall think themselves accursed they were not here,
> And hold their manhoods cheap whiles any speaks
> That fought with us upon Saint Crispin's day.'

Easy to imagine its impact on an impressionable thirteen-year-old boy seeing it for the first time so soon after D Day. The doughty English had triumphed at Agincourt and done so yet again on the Normandy beaches. 'Cry God for Harry, England and St George!' Good rousing stuff.

Little was left of Agincourt now except the battlefield but Honfleur, further away on the Normandy coast, looked much more promising and I vaguely remembered something in Shakespeare about Henry besieging Honfleur en route to Agincourt. With its narrow medieval streets of half-timbered buildings and its historic main square, it looked like an interesting place. 'Not necessarily after a ferry crossing in December,' my daughters pointed out. 'Oh come on!' I said, 'You're young. Live dangerously for once. Lots of people are planning all kinds of mad things for the Millennium. This is tame by comparison.' It wasn't.

Getting there at all was an achievement in the face of many obstacles in the form of delays, cancelled ferries, gale force winds and driving rain. Things started off smoothly enough with a drive down from Leeds the day before. We were staying with friends in Lewes from where we'd catch the Newhaven to Dieppe ferry the next morning. Matt and Emilia had already suggested it was cheaper for us all to take one car and had arranged to pick us up early. Nerissa and her new boyfriend had opted for Eurostar to Calais and then a hired car to do the longish drive down to Honfleur.

But the next morning, we woke to a terrific storm that had built up in the night. Gale-force winds tore at the trees beyond the garden and the rain was sheeting down. Emilia and Matt were late picking us up because of a fallen tree on the A23. There seemed little chance of a ferry crossing at all given the weather conditions. When we reached the port entrance there was a steel barrier across it and a poor girl from P&O Ferries, holding on to her uniform hat for dear life, left the shelter of her glass pillbox to advise us what to do. At that very moment the wind picked up the steel barrier and smashed it into the glass door behind her giving her a lucky escape. Nothing was leaving from Newhaven she told us unnecessarily. We might try the 10.00 a.m. ferry from Folkestone; there was a possibility that might be sailing.

Folkestone would mean the Calais route and no one was happy about the possibility of a three-hour-drive on top of what might be a rough ferry crossing but there was nothing for it except to give it a try. Rather than risk a return trip up the A23, we decided to go the coastal route, which was probably a mistake. East Sussex into Kent is a long and tedious journey and by the time we reached Hastings, Emilia and I were desperate for the loo. This meant a detour along the deserted seafront where a wild ocean was crashing at the sea wall. When we found the conveniences we both made a blind run for them with them our heads down against the wind. We'd not been back in the car for long when an unmistakable smell announced we'd both skidded into the same pile of dog shit. There was no end of a fuss about this from Jim and Matt. We were made to stamp about on a grass verge in the rain and only allowed back in the car after a careful shoe inspection. Misery was setting in. At Folkestone, hardly surprisingly, we heard the 10.00 a.m. ferry was cancelled due to 'inclement weather'. 'Come back at 1.00 p.m.,' we were told. A ferry might be running then. That meant three hours to kill in the pouring rain in Folkestone which wasn't a happy prospect. We went our separate ways with Jim and I taking shelter in a Waterstone's until the staff became curious about us and we felt we had to leave. Forlornly we wandered in and out of several charity shops looking for a coffee shop. Nothing seemed open in December as we tramped about getting wetter and wetter. Eventually, on an unlikely side street, we saw a café sign and made a beeline for it. As we got nearer the first thing we saw through its steamed-up windows was Matt and Emilia tucking into a full English breakfast. Hard not to feel left out somehow. Hard not to feel resentful that they were warm and dry. At this point, coming up to eleven o'clock, someone, not me, had the bright idea (I didn't have a mobile phone in those days) of ringing the ferry company and finding out if there would be a sailing at 1.00 p.m. No, there would not, but the weather forecast for the next day was better and if we presented ourselves at Newhaven in the morning our original booking would be honoured.

Well, this was all going extraordinarily well. Now everyone was looking at me. There was nothing for it but to return to Brighton. 'At least we won't have that long drive after the ferry crossing now,' I said. No one answered me. Despondency was setting in fast. How could I rally spirits? 'Look,' I said, 'if we have to go back to Brighton we could all stay at The Old Ship Hotel on the seafront and go out for dinner in that wonderful fish restaurant next door.' Matt and Emilia looked a little hesitant; 'On our tab of course,' I said. They beamed; Jim raised his eyebrows.

Somehow or other we did get a sailing the next day in slightly better weather and then began the sixty-mile drive from Dieppe to Honfleur across flat, flat, country that felt at times as if we were aquaplaning some vast runway that would never end. Matt was beginning to lose confidence in me altogether and I didn't blame him. We weren't even there yet, and by now I knew, from a telephone call, that Nerissa and the boyfriend, Mike, had also had a bad journey. Their Eurotunnel crossing had been cancelled because of the bad weather and they had had to stay in a Premier Inn near Gatwick Airport. Currently, they were driving to Honfleur in a hire car after an early morning flight to Paris. Costs were mounting up all round and whose fault was it? No one seemed to think it was the weather.

Finally we were there, twenty-four hours later than intended. I waited for the first person to say a trip to France in winter was a daft idea. They didn't need to, all the looks said it anyway when we met up in a bistro overlooking the main square. Greetings were distinctly damp and weary. I'd never met Mike before, and my first impressions were of a bleary-eyed young man huddled up in a duffle coat with the hood up, wearing sun glasses. The first thing Nerissa said to me, after an initial hello, was to ask if I had any paracetamol for him. Apparently they'd drowned their sorrows lavishly the night before and now he was nursing a terrible hangover after a bumpy flight. Wasn't this going well? I'd wanted everyone to have some fun, particularly Nerissa. Three years back from New York, she'd had a tough time re-establishing herself in a West London advertising agency and done very well, but it had left little time for weekend breaks: this was supposed to be it.

At least there was a Christmas fair in full swing and a few fireworks in the evening when the Christmas lights were switched on but it was still bitterly cold. We were glad to dive back to the *pension* and huddle round a log fire. After a good dinner, everyone's spirits were revived a little as we drank more Calvados and took it in turns to say what we hoped the twenty-first century might bring. Now I had another problem. I'd come with some souvenirs to give to everyone to mark the occasion. The giant stainless-steel kitchen spoons I'd bought, seemed a good, practical idea. I knew they would last and their everyday use would be a nice reminder of the Millennium and the place where we'd gathered together, but I had made the mistake of taking them for engraving to a place that specialised in football trophies. 'Honfleur' and 'Millennium' in one engraving in italic script was a challenge too far for the shop that would happily have coped with 'Batley' or 'Heckmondwike' or 'Cleckheaton'. When I went to collect them I saw they said 'Milennium 2000 at Honfleur' in a horrible, bold font that looked as if it had come off a baked beans tin and would, I knew, attract comment. That wasn't the worst of it; I only had three spoons. One for us, one for Matt and Emilia and one for Nerissa. Mike, a current, not a permanent boyfriend, as I had been reliably informed, was a late inclusion to the party. No etiquette could cover the situation. Did I give him the spoon intended for Jim and myself, which was tantamount to saying I knew he wouldn't be around for long or did I pretend his long weekends with Nerissa in her cottage in Kew indicated they were one household? The latter seemed the only way to go but in my embarrassment as I handed them out I started prattling on about the symbolism of steel, time passing, the bonds of family in their generations and the importance of our all being together and other nonsense that had Nerissa and Emilia groaning with familiarity. At least the moment passed off reasonably well. We all sat back and refilled our glasses. This was the moment I think Jim had been waiting for. 'So,' he said as he took a worn Penguin copy of *Henry V* from his pocket, 'here we all are, by one means or another, in Honfleur where Henry V first landed before he fought his battle at Agincourt and where he said these famous lines', and he began to read:

> 'Once more unto the breach,
> Dear friends, once more;
> Or close the wall up with our English dead…'

Then he stopped. 'What is it?' I said. He looked down at the text. 'I've just noticed what it says at the top of the scene.' 'Well, what does it say?' I asked. 'Read it for yourself,' he said and shoved the book at me. I looked down at the page in puzzlement. 'Go on,' Jim said. 'Out loud. So everyone can hear. Read the stage direction.' This was getting tiresome. 'All right,' I said. 'Enter the King, Bedford and Gloucester. Alarum: Scaling ladders at Harfleur.' Then I stopped too. 'What's that word you just read?' 'Harfleur,' I said. 'Exactly,' Jim pounced. 'Harfleur. Not Honfleur.' The others looked on puzzled. 'They're the same thing,' I said. 'Just Elizabethan spelling.' 'No, of course they're not,' Jim said. 'How could I have been so stupid. I knew perfectly well about the siege of Harfleur. Harfleur and Honfleur are two separate towns either side of the Seine estuary.' There was complete silence then Mike said, 'Does this mean we're in the wrong place?' 'Yes, it does,' Jim said. 'Henry besieged Harfleur before going on to Agincourt, not Honfleur.' 'So what's special about this place?' Nerissa asked. 'Nothing,' said Jim, 'Just your mother's conviction. More fool me for me for not checking up on it beforehand. I might have known she'd get it wrong.' They all looked at me accusingly. 'I'm sorry. I'm sorry,' I said. How would I ever live it down? We'd had all the problems of getting there in winter and then I'd compounded it all with a big steel spoon to stir things up that would for ever say 'Honfleur' not 'Harfleur' in a ghastly script. I wished I could disappear as I waited for the storm to burst over my head. 'It's quite a nice place anyway,' Nerissa said kindly. 'And it must be near the other place,' Matt said. Jim grudgingly had to agree with that. Emilia picked her spoon up and said, 'At least we won't ever forget we came to the wrong place. Well done Mum. You've excelled yourself this time.' And suddenly they were all waving their spoons at me and laughing. I could see this one would run and run for a long time. 'What did *you* do for the Millennium?' Yeah. Yeah. What we actually did for the Millennium was celebrate it in our family's own, daft way.

Nothing in fact marked the new century for me as much as the arrival of the next generation. My first grandson Freddie was born in 2001 with perfect timing in the week's break I had while on tour with *The Importance of Being Earnest*, in which I was playing Miss Prism. In view of the debacle I made of Honfleur and other episodes in my life it might be said that there was some typecasting going on here. Given the right circumstances I was quite capable of leaving a baby in a handbag at Victoria Station, on or off stage, and provided anecdotal evidence to back it up.

This was a very alternative production of the play. Not a word in the text was changed but the whole was a glorious vehicle for the celebrated comedy duo of Maggie Fox and Sue Ryding, who, as 'Lip Service Theatre', had a stream of literary and artistic spoofs behind them that had brought them a well-earned cult following. Their input, combined with Lawrence Till's inspired direction, resulted in a wild extravaganza loved by the audience. In the course of the three acts Maggie played Jack Worthing and Lady Bracknell and Sue played Algernon and Cecily with all the rest of the parts being transgender cast except Miss Prism. The set-up for all this was shared with the audience before the play began when Maggie Fox explained that half the company had been detained at the local police station, and that, rather than wait for them to arrive, we thought we better get started by taking on each other's parts. She backed this up by showing off Jack Worthing's jacket that she was now wearing instead of Gwendolen's frock. Other cast members showed their equal willingness to help out by gesturing to their 'new' costumes, all except Miss Prism. The fun here was that I was an old school actress, who, dressed in a silk dressing gown and turban, reminiscent of another age, refused to be a part of such nonsense, saying, 'I have been contracted to play Miss Prism and that's all I am prepared to play,' before marching resolutely back to the dressing room.

The show was to open at Watford Palace Theatre with the technical dress rehearsal the day before. A tech day can be long and tedious as the lighting plot is being set and various lanterns repositioned. This, combined with setting the level for audio cues, can mean the opening sequence of any play is often the trickiest to set but all went off fairly smoothly on this occasion in under fifty minutes. As Miss Prism, I left the stage in a huff to march back to my dressing room; except I went the wrong way. Instead of going stage left as I'd been told to do, I marched off stage right oblivious of my mistake. For several minutes I groped about in semi-darkness. Because the back wall of the set came right up against the back wall of the stage, there was literally no entrance from stage right to stage left and I needed to get back to the dressing room to put on my full costume for Miss Prism. Not to worry. Surely there was a way round the problem through the scene dock? The forty-feet-high scene dock doors were open and I slipped in past the paint shop to a sliding door at the far end that surely connected to the rest of the building. It didn't and now the door I'd come through had clanged shut decisively behind me. Slightly panicking, I found myself on a path that ran the entire outside length of the building. Several metal emergency doors, of the sort you see in cinemas, were set into it. No good trying them from the outside, I knew they opened only one way. I tried battering on them with my arms but some scene change music was being played at such a high volume that no one could hear me. Help! Did this mean they'd reached Scene Two and I'd be off? I ran down the rest of the path that brought me to the front of the theatre at street level. Through its locked glass doors I could see the entire foyer area was empty. I bent down and tried to shout through the hinges. 'Hello. Can somebody let me in please?' At this precise moment an Arriva service bus drew up at the bus stop outside. I turned round to see some passengers pointing me out and laughing. I truly must have looked like some demented clown. The wardrobe mistress's inspired final touch was to add to my costume some bright pink, furry bedroom slippers, of the kind an older actress might wear for comfort in the dressing room. There I stood, slippers and all, in a Noel Coward-style dressing gown and tiger print turban, alternately waving my arms about and banging on the foyer doors. I was nearly crying and by now the bus was tilting as more passengers crowded to one side to gawp at me through the windows. This was not going to end well. Back I ran to the emergency doors and tried battering and shouting through them once more. Mercifully someone heard me this time. There was the sound of the safety bar being lifted but the doors opening suddenly took me so completely by surprise that I fell straightforward on to my face and lay there panting. The whole auditorium of technicians, lighting crew, director, stage management and fellow actors let out great whoops of laughter that only ended when Lawrence Till called for an early tea break to settle everyone down. From then on I was consigned a minder to get me off and on the stage for the next three weeks: an indignity I suffered in silence.

The arrival of Freddie into all of this was an enormous joy. Nothing could adequately describe my feelings as I held him in my arms, eight hours after he was born. As the mother of two daughters I was thrilled to have a grandson.

Foetal scans that could determine the baby's sex were not routinely on offer during either of my pregnancies. If they had been, although I'm not naturally a patient person, I think I would have waited for the excitement of the birth to find out if I had a son or daughter, even though a scan might have saved me some heart-searching. I had promised my father, in agreement with Jim, that if I had sons I would have them circumcised; in fact I would have wanted it myself but once again dithered around with doubts to my entitlement. My mother's conversion before the Liberal Beth Din gave her the same rights and responsibilities under Jewish law as if she was born Jewish. Accordingly, through her *ketubah* (Jewish marriage certificate) these passed to me too and to my daughters but I wrestled with the knowledge that Orthodox Judaism does not accept conversions authorised through Liberal Judaism. Was I fish or fowl? If I applied intellectual rigour to the question I could see the Orthodox point of view; a Jew is a child born of a Jewish mother born of a Jewish mother in a long line of continuation. As ever I was in judgement on myself: what was I? Potentially my pregnancy was pressing me for my own answer. If I had a son the ceremony should take place on the eighth day; I would need to decide things in advance. Taking a deep breath I asked my father if he would arrange the *bris* (circumcision) if I had a son and he had agreed. With the arrival of daughters the matter could be forgotten. Now I had a grandson; in fact I was to be blessed with another four grandsons over the next five years when Freddie was joined two years later by his brother Robert, within twelve months of which, Nerissa, on her marriage to Adam, had her first son Alec and then Sam and lastly baby Bruno. This was family in its next generation, but at none of these arrivals was a *bris* ever mentioned by me. By inheritance and cultural influence the growing family was partly Jewish and partly English and partly Polish through my son-in-law, Adam, whose father was a Pole who fought with the British Army. A consequence of my own mixed marriage was the increasing secularisation of my daughters as they began building their own families away from any influence of mine. I saw that practising my Judaism now became increasingly my own private affair which I needed to balance within my marriage in order not to cause division with Jim and with my daughters who had never had the chance to understand how thorough my upbringing in Judaism had been: a certain amount of loneliness, in this respect, would be inherent for me in the years ahead.

Chapter 12
BEING EARNEST

My eldest grandson invented his own name for me. On my frequent visits to see him in Surrey he would listen to the stream of commonplace exchanges I had with his mother and hear them as 'Meelie [Emilia's family nickname], shall I bring the washing in?'; 'Meelie, what time do I need to be ready?'; 'Meelie, shall I take that upstairs?' One day, aged around two-and-a-half, he pointed to me and called me 'Meelar'. The concept of it being his mother's name was beyond his understanding. Clearly I must be self-identifying as someone called Meelar with all my utterances, 'I, Meelar, shall I bring the washing in?' 'I, Meelar, what time do I need to be ready?' 'I, Meelar shall I take that upstairs?' but the name has stuck; at least in private. I formed the picture in my head long ago of some ancient Russian retainer wandering in from a Chekhov play, with her feet bound in cloth bandages to put on the samovar. At least Freddie had the excuse of imperfect understanding. I had no excuse for careless inattention which I could be accused of on several occasions.

I had written a play whose theme had haunted me for a long time. At drama school I'd known a shy girl who came from Derbyshire; let's call her Simone. Simone lacked confidence in herself; what little self-esteem she did possess was constantly being eroded by her very successful, much older sister Lesley, who was a highly successful model with a glamorous lifestyle in a swish apartment in St John's Wood. Simone was regularly being summonsed to cocktail parties there, where she agonised with me over what to wear. Whatever she came up with on her limited budget was ridiculed by Lesley in front of all her glamorous friends. No doubt Lesley thought it was only friendly banter but Simone took it very hard. I'd talk with her about the party after the event and try to persuade her to refuse the next invitation; she never did. Instead, I'd see her worried little face as she set off in her grey duffle coat with her long, straight, light brown hair held back by a crimson velvet Alice band. After drama school she made a hasty marriage to an actor who beat her up, tried to get into the theatre and failed, became deeply anorexic and ended up living on her own as a secretary at Granada Television in Manchester where I was now living out on the Cheshire side. We spoke several times on the telephone and several times she arranged to come out and see me as I jostled life with a newborn baby. For one reason or another, these meetings were always cancelled by her at the last minute and eventually I gave up trying to arrange anything. Several months later I was utterly devastated to learn Simone had died of untreated anorexia and self-neglect at only twenty-five and she had not been found for several days. How could I not have known she was so desperately unhappy and mentally ill? Could I, should I, have done more? The horror, the waste and pity of it threatened to overwhelm me and I have never forgotten her. At every turn in my life I think of her and have angry conversations with her in my head asking her why she didn't seek help. 'Look at everything you've missed,' I say. 'You too could have found a good man eventually, built a family; enjoyed a career; seen your grandchildren arrive.'

The play she inspired is a confrontation between a middle-aged woman, Marie, and her ghost friend, Simone, on the eve of Marie's daughter's big white wedding. As other characters busy themselves in the details of the wedding day, Marie – half in anguish, half in despair – asks Simone for answers but the forever young, mercurial Simone is playful and much more bent on squeezing herself into the wedding photographs and trying on the bride's headdress. When she does talk of the past it's to conjure up the fun they once shared together, dancing round their handbags in some disco while the music of the sixties went on and on and on as they sang along to it at the top of their voices.

I started the play with this image from the past of the girls singing raucously along to the music and called the play, *Bye, Bye Miss America High*. It had a nice plug in the *Radio Times* the week before but it wasn't until we got into the studio and had recorded the first scene that the floor manager said to me conversationally as she set up the props for the next scene, 'Why did you call the play *Bye, Bye Miss America High*?' I looked at her as if she was stupid. 'Because it's the name of the song,' I said, 'The song they're singing at the opening. Bye, Bye Miss America High. Drove my chevy to the levy but the levy was dry.' Everyone looked at me and then the sound engineer shook his head in disbelief, 'The song is called "American Pie",' he said. 'No,' I said, 'It can't be; that's just not possible.' 'It is,' they all chorused. 'So why has no one told me before?' I demanded. They all looked at my appalled face and started laughing. I couldn't find anything funny in it all. 'It's in the *Radio Times* now,' I said and felt myself going red with shame. 'What did you think it meant then?' the director asked me. I didn't. With supreme confidence I had merely reproduced what I thought I'd heard and what I'd heard was a lament about loss in which the words had not seemed to matter. 'I thought you were being enigmatic and clever,' the director went on. 'That there was some subtle pun on words going on here.' I shook my head. 'No,' I said. I was simply being inattentive and careless but I couldn't admit to that. Worse was to come. The reviews were very favourable and as I picked up each one I had to suffer the same humiliation. 'Bye, Bye Miss America High' they were all headed. Finally the play was short-listed for the BAFTA Mental Health Drama Award and I had to sit and squirm in my seat as the title was pronounced in confident tones by responsible people in evening dress who all looked as if they knew what it meant.

I came home from the awards ceremony with my tail between my legs, feeling foolish but the support from the other side of the kitchen table reminded me I wasn't the only one in this household who got into situations. We opened a bottle of wine and glumly swapped stories. Jim won hands down. Things had a way of happening to him willy-nilly. One of his best scrapes was the time he was mistaken for another Mr Walsh, an important wine merchant, flying into Bordeaux Airport as a guest of Monsieur Martel. Flushed with his recent appointment as registrar of the university, and on his way to a high-profile European conference on university education, Jim thought it entirely appropriate, as he told me to his shame, that a uniformed chauffeur should hold up a card on his arrival that said 'Mr Walsh' and ask him to '*suivez*' out to a waiting Mercedes. Not until they had been driving for over twenty minutes and the car had already swept over the Garonne and Gironde rivers and out into the open countryside, did he vaguely begin to wonder why the guest accommodation for the conference was so far outside the city. On, on they drove as the afternoon sunlight turned into evening until the Mercedes crunched up a long, gravel drive to deposit him outside Château Cantenac, the home of Monsieur Martel, whose English agent was on the steps to greet him. He was shown to a palatial room where a cold supper was laid out for him and after a comfortable night, in a bed with silk sheets, was woken early by heavy pounding on the door. The same agent, now clearly very agitated, asked him who he was and at the end of the explanation said, 'There has been a terrible mistake. Where are you supposed to be?' The answer, at a European conference on university education in Bordeaux Trois only bewildered the poor man even more. No one mentioned what had happened to the Mr Walsh who had been expected, who was presumably still stranded at Bordeaux Airport. The agent went off and made some telephone calls, then came back. 'A car will take you back to the city,' he said. 'If you'd like to leave *now* it will be waiting outside for you.' No Mercedes this time, no uniformed chauffeur either. A small Renault, driven by a man in blue overalls, trundled back the way they'd come the previous evening to deposit Jim at the conference in Bordeaux Trois, which was already in full session with the first speech of the day. His colleagues hooted when they saw him, not believing a word of his explanation. Clearly he'd been on some dalliance of his own that their discretion stopped them from enquiring about any further but the story joined others told about him on many occasions.

On a much earlier occasion, before I knew him, setting out on the first day of his holiday in a new car, he'd picked up an art student hitch-hiker on the outskirts of Manchester who'd asked him how far he was going and received the swaggering reply from Jim, 'To Rome' to which the student had replied, 'That's brilliant, mate. I'm going to Brindisi to catch the ferry to Greece.' Apparently a negotiation was made under duress that Jim would take the boy as far as Dover but the end result was the boy had a free ride as far as Termini Station in Rome because Jim, though thoroughly fed up with him by then, hadn't the heart to evict him once he learned that the boy only had the equivalent of £20 to take him across France and down through Italy. For his pains he received a slap on the shoulder and the promise of 'A pint, mate, if I ever bump into you again back in Manchester.'

Becoming computer literate in the late 1990s gave Jim a new toy. Once he had mastered basic word processing skills sufficient to aid his ongoing serious work for prestigious publishers like Minerva and *History Today*, he turned his delight to the attractions of email, beginning a daily blog that he sent to his retired registrar chums on any number of subjects that took his fancy. A fairly typical piece about his pet hates got taken up by his friend Brian MacArthur, and published in *Times 2* under the heading, "'Ten Things I Hate About Now' by my good friend James Walsh of Leeds".

> People who throw things out of cars.
> Rap music from open-windowed cars.
> 'Get out of my way' flash headlights.
> People who put at least twenty-five articles on the ten-only aisle at supermarket checkouts.
> Instruction booklets for PCs.
> People who drink out of bottles in pubs.
> Waiters who say, 'Enjoy your meal'.
> Waiters who ask, 'Will you be having the Chardonnay?'
> Taxi drivers who talk.

Another of his pet hates was mispronunciation. Tesco's was his stalking ground, as well as his favourite information zone. Always with tongue in cheek and a twinkle in his eye, he decided one day to do some personal research there into the pronunciation of the letter 'H' and equipped himself with a small card with the letter 'H' in capitals on it. Two of the girls on the checkouts, who knew him well, seemed mystified but complied; a couple of customers thought he was crackers and refused to answer but overall, he reported in his blog, that he got a fairly good response from which he dolefully concluded that the battle was over and 'haitch' was now the accepted pronunciation.

Essentially at seventy-four his health was good with only mild concern ever expressed over an enlarged prostate for which he had an annual check-up with one of his consultant chums whom he knew well from the medical school. But that summer when he came home from his routine overhaul his first words to me were, 'We could be in trouble.' The consultant radiographer had seen an anomaly on the scan as he checked the kidneys: a potential aortic aneurysm. His advice to Jim was that he should see a vascular consultant fairly soon.

This wasn't good news; both Jim's father and grandfather had died of a burst aortic aneurysm that had gone undetected. There was family history here.

A fortnight later the diagnosis was confirmed and a planned intervention put in place. Because this was major surgery, received wisdom was to delay the operation for as long as possible until the measurement of the potential aneurysm suggested the timing was ripe for intervention. From September to April, Jim was carefully monitored in a waiting game and we, almost successfully, put the whole thing to one side. There were good distractions like Emilia's wedding in December attended by Freddie and Robbie in the way things were now done, and the joyful news of Nerissa's first pregnancy. Six years after her divorce she had met Adam and was looking forward to their life together and with Alec's arrival in the March the seal was set on their happiness.

The surgery following in April was long and the time in

intensive care afterwards gave cause for twenty-four hours of nail-biting anxiety but, as the post-operative days increased in number, there was room for optimism as well as relief that the operation had been a success. Convalescence was slow, if steady, and as the spring advanced Jim gradually recovered ground. By July we took a week's holiday in Majorca: a recently discovered destination after years of being incredibly snobby about the place based on nothing other than hearsay and prejudice. By December a commission of mine to adapt a classic Swedish novel took us to Stockholm for a long weekend. Perhaps the following summer we might think of a return to Greece or even further afield.

Chapter 13
TWILIGHT

With hindsight, and mercifully so, I later learned that the survival rate after aortic repair surgery is three to five years. We had three. The vascular disease, first evident in the abdominal aorta, began to show itself elsewhere in the body. Jim's walking gradually became worse and worse. Always pragmatic, he had no false pride in accepting a mobility scooter for days out, particularly if the grandsons were visiting when he'd swing them aboard with him and race them through the Wakefield Sculpture Park or through a theme park on a family get-together in Witney. But he grew frailer and frailer and moved about with difficulty, only feeling really safe at home. Our world was becoming more and more circumscribed but it was precious, as if we both tacitly knew that time was finite and to be measured in days not years. On one occasion we had a seemingly jokey conversation about funerals in which he managed to tell me what hymns he'd like and we discussed a choice between a reading of Dylan Thomas's 'Fern Hill' and W H Auden's 'As I Walked Out One Evening' but concluded the Auden was ultimately pessimistic and I told him that, notwithstanding his professed atheism, I knew through and through that any ritual attached to his departing belonged with the prayers and cadences of the *King James Bible* and *The Book of Common Prayer* that had defined him from the beginning as a traditional Englishman.

In January 2008 he had an emergency admission to hospital with a suggested strangulated bowel, which caused a massive heart attack that he didn't survive. My whole world collapsed. Twenty when I met him, for over forty-four years we'd been indivisible. Who was I without him? My grief was too deep for tears.

His Church of England funeral had a massive attendance. He was loved and enjoyed by so many for his humanity and his kindness and his fun. His friend Emrys Wyn Jones from Aberystwyth read 'Fern Hill' beautifully, bringing his own Welsh tunes to the lines and as I listened the very words seemed to describe all the joy we had had in our long marriage from the beginning.

'All the sun long it was running, it was lovely, the hay
Fields high as the house, the tunes from the chimneys, it was air
And playing, lovely and watery
And fire green as grass.'

For nearly forty-one years, life had been like a running stream between us, full of movement, laughter, lightness, sunlight on changing shapes, hilarity, stillness, rants, opinions, anecdotes, stories, jokes, his endless fund of quotations that he summoned up from somewhere. Jim was well known for them. Words delighted him all his life and their careless or inaccurate use in any public piece of writing was likely to gain a response. It was entirely fitting that Brian MacArthur's eulogy made reference to this love of words. He let Jim speak for himself, choosing to read out one of Jim's most recent email exchanges that encapsulated much of his fun and his wit.

'November 12 2004

Email from: J J Walsh To: Sam Leith, Literary Editor of the *Daily Telegraph*

Subject: Standards of English

Dear Sam Leith, In today's edition, p 22, col 1, you refer to Niall Ferguson "careening" down a US highway. I grow a little weary of writing to *Telegraph* and *Times* journalists explaining the difference between the verbs "to career" and "to careen". If you look at the *Concise Oxford Dictionary* you will see the two meanings placed conveniently together. "Career" – of a horse etc., a short gallop at full speed, "careen" – to turn a ship over on one side for cleaning, caulking or repairing.

Yours sincerely, J J Walsh.

November 12 2004

Email from: Sam Leith. To: J J Walsh

Subject: Re Standards of English

Dear Mr Walsh, It was the image of turning on to one side, Wacky-Races-style, that I had in mind. I'm sorry you're getting weary. You'd save much energy if you didn't write.

Yours sincerely, Sam Leith.

Email to Sam Leith from J J Walsh

Dear Sam Leith,

"There's glory for you," said Humpty Dumpty.

"I don't know what you mean," said Alice.

"Of course you don't until I tell you what it means," said Humpty Dumpty. "What I mean is –'there's a nice knock-down argument for you.'"

"The question is," said Alice, "whether you can make a word to

mean what you want it to mean."
"The question is," said Humpty Dumpty, "Who is to be master. That's all."
J J W

Email to J J Walsh from Sam Leith
Dear Mr Walsh,
It's a fair cop.
You win, Sam Leith.'

The church was filled with affectionate laughter. For many it was as if Jim was amongst us but for me it was the start of a kind of emotional paralysis. I was frozen into my own grief. The days that followed are a blank in my memory. The first spring came and I never noticed it nor the summer that followed. I took trains to see friends, visited new places, refused no invitations, or so my diary tells me but I've no picture in my head of myself moving through any of those situations. The diary records the date and time of each appointment and I read back through it all with bemusement. Who was the she who did these things while I was somewhere else? Yet it was me who dealt efficiently with financial and administrative matters. It was me who helped plan the large memorial service that the university gave for Jim in the autumn. And me who did some professional work. I don't remember the details of any of it. I do know I became fanatical about controlling my immediate physical environment to the point of complete irrationality: a metaphor no doubt for the 'out of control' state inside my head. Every letter had to be dealt with immediately, each task had to be performed by a certain hour, no stray newspaper, sock, paper bag, dead leaf could lie about without my pouncing on it. By the following winter I was exhausted with an alarmingly high blood pressure. The GP sent me off to a cardiac consultant who, after the usual tests of ECG and a twenty-four-hour monitoring of my blood pressure, obtained via a beeping contraption strapped round my middle, wrote to reassure me it was 'only grief'. I stared at the words, or rather at the one word, 'only'. How easy. How unthinking. Some anger kicked in, maybe it was helpful. You're on your own here, pal, I thought. No one understands. No one at all. There was only one person who would have done but he wasn't there. How unfair was that when I needed to talk to him more than anything in the world? Without even thinking of the illogicality of it all I sat down to write him a letter and as I wrote I felt calmer, as if he was listening to me in another place.

March 28 2009

My Dearest Jim,

You can't know how I long to talk to you. Just once. Just for a few minutes. That's not a lot to ask, is it? Since January 2008 I've not had a conversation with anyone that came within a whisper of what we shared so it's a lonely place to be left in by myself. How can I believe that only twelve days after that conversation I would be attending your funeral? And yes, it did go well. A packed send-off as they say. You would have been pleased about that. And yes, Emrys did read the Dylan Thomas, and he did it beautifully. I've looked at it so often since then.

And honoured among foxes and pheasants by the gay house
Under the new-made clouds and happy as the heart was long
In the sun born over and over
I ran my heedless ways.

It was your childhood in Barrowford as much as Thomas's in Swansea, wasn't it? I always knew that. Riding the hay cart on Leo Begley's farm, cycling under the thick canopy of overhanging trees that dappled Blacko Lane, walking up Pendle Hill with the church banners on Good Friday. And all of it lived out in the intensity of those war years that I could never catch up with and possess as common ground between us, try as I might; and now I never will.

Your death is like a bar line coming down in a piece of music, cutting everything off abruptly. What I thought was infinite is finite; it started and now it's ended. It made me go back to the beginning of us, the images so clear in my head, like a still from a film. You are there at that New Year's Eve party in 1964, propped up against the fireplace in your brown suede jacket ready to shock me. 'I sell *The Daily Worker* on street corners,' you said. 'And I'm divorced.' But give me credit. I knew something was special about you even then. They say that love is the attraction of opposites and there was much in us that fitted that description but there was also much that was essentially the same. Ourselves against the world. Two outsiders, each soulmate to the other. Myself in flight from the rejection that orthodox Judaism had made on my mother's conversion and ultimately on me; yourself in flight from a working-class background. We each needed something from the other; I your unshakeable sense of identity, you my middle-class confidence. Our marriage was the collaboration of two cultures into something liberating and idiosyncratic and outside the mainstream. We were each other's safe haven so that it's a lonely place to be left in by myself. I miss you so much. You have no idea. The clocks went forwards last night and you weren't here. Spring forwards. Fall back. You

179

always got it wrong and had to ring the speaking clock, do you remember? And even then you'd get into a muddle with re-winding the Grandfather clock and get cross. 'Darling, what is the time now?' you'd shout out. Did you think the equinox had brought an extension to the usual twenty-four? Thinking about it, you'd a whole vocabulary of 'darlings' that you used on different occasions. I can hear them now in my head. There was 'Dah-ling! Where are you?' – the playful, domestic one you sang up the stairs. There was 'Darling' – the simple truth between us. And then the conciliatory and coaxing 'Dar-l-inggg!' to bring me round after you'd had that extra drink and I objected. Or the peremptory and annoyed 'DarlinG!' – with the Lancastrian hard 'g' back in place. ' DarlinG! When will you ever learn to put the tops on things? I've just walked into the kitchen and picked up the Nescafe jar only to have the lot spew out across the floor. Do you never think?' you'd say. Well, I wasn't the only one. Your forgetfulness was legendary. Car keys, glasses, cheques, bills, your finally completed MA thesis on a tram so legend has it. Once you forgot your house key so I pinned you a note to the back door to explain where I'd left it, do you remember that? 'La clef est dans le garage,' I wrote. When I came back there was another note pinned there by you. 'Wanted. Reliable thief with good knowledge of work-a-day French,' it said. Oh, you were such fun. But you were many other things, as well: the serious thinker with the broad ideas, the life-enhancer, the worrier, the wit; also a kind and fair man with a decency and simplicity I envied. Enthusiasm. Zest. Participation. I try to focus on those qualities, but always I keep getting stuck on the horror of your ending. How could you have done this without me? How could that body I knew so well, each freckle, mole, finger nail, earlobe have moved into that other space and left me by myself? I try consciously to find a picture – ourselves on the Rialto Bridge in Venice where you sang to me, being impossibly bossed by you as you skippered a motor boat across the bay in Greece, a drink on the terrace of the Sydney Opera House, a meal in Sebastopol, sand castles in Devon, seal-sightings in Scotland, all the things we shared, but always my head returns and returns to that night and to the question I most want to ask you: 'How do I go on without you?'

After I had finished writing I felt calmer and I wept. Clean tears. Clean grief. No regrets. No unfinished business. Just the aching starkness of loss.

By this time I had acquired a cat, or rather he had acquired me. He'd wandered through the back door three weeks before Jim died and had made himself at home. Jim quickly took to him and named him Monty but said he didn't want to get too fond of him in case he left again. Ironically it wasn't the cat that was leaving three weeks later which, in hindsight, made his arrival poignant. Scrupulously I'd tried to find out if he was really homeless. Had he been chipped? Did he need vaccinating? Worming? Generally speaking I preferred dogs to cats. It's not that I didn't like cats, I just never saw the point of them like dogs, but for the first fourteen months of my widowhood he kept me company, though very much on his own terms. Jet black with green eyes, he was perfect casting as a witch's familiar and something about his character matched the role. Aloof, demanding, not particularly affectionate, he nevertheless was a focus needing to be fed and watered every day. His appetite was enormous and after yet another meal he'd bang off out through the cat flap to sit on the outside kitchen windowsill and stare back at me through the glass. His only real emotion was jealousy if the two eldest grandsons were visiting, when he'd bite their ankles behind my back and send them screaming from the room; also, he was a coward. Prone to chasing birds of course; if he seemed to be on the losing side of a large blackbird or similar, he'd corner them by chasing them back through the cat flap for me to deal with in the kitchen. One day he definitely took on more than he could chew and I turned round to find a vicious-looking grey squirrel in the kitchen. The poor thing was baring its teeth because it was panicking but so was I. Close to, there's no way you can throw a tea towel over a squirrel and then grab it to release it back into the open. First the squirrel jumped on to the windowsill and it and Monty eyed each through the glass with Monty visibly trembling. Then it jumped on to the pine dresser and from there on to the kitchen work surface. In every place it left a pile of shit. I ran out into the hall crying, 'I can't cope with this. I can't.' No one answered me. No one was going to answer me. Of course not, somehow it was up to me. Cautiously I went back into the kitchen and after opening the back door, got hold of two wooden trays. I waited until the squirrel had jumped down to the floor and then put a tea tray either side of it to trap it into a V-shaped funnel. Unable to see anywhere but straight ahead, I was able then to edge it in a dragging action towards the back door. Miraculously it took the exit route on offer and I was left with an entire kitchen to disinfect, but more than that. The realisation came to me in that moment of triumph: I was on my own and I had coped and I could and would cope because I had to.

Work forced me through the first months. Shortly after the funeral I was performing in Goole in a new play, a two hander, put on through the theatre company that I had formed with two fellow actors four years before called 'Yellow Leaf Theatre'. The name came from the opening of Shakespeare's Sonnet 73.

> That time of year thou mayst in me behold
> When yellow leaves, or none, or few, do hang
> Upon those boughs which shake against the cold,
> Bare ruin'd choirs, where late the sweet birds sang.

Our aim in setting up the company was to foster new drama that explored the concerns and disappointments of the over-fifties age group and to take the productions to towns and rural villages that seldom saw live theatre. The Arts Council then were keen on this kind of initiative and gave us a small grant. Over a couple of seasons we had had some good reviews, both for the new writing and for the ethos of the company itself that resulted in an article about us in *Times 2* supplement. Audience figures had been building but they were not in evidence on a cold Saturday in winter in Goole. I remember walking round and round the fish docks in a state of unreality wondering how on earth I could step on stage and perform in a couple of hours. There is a physical dimension to grief. No one tells you how exhausted you feel all the time; your energy levels are on the floor. Somehow I must have got by on autopilot and with the discipline instilled in me down the years; I was much in need of it. An even greater task awaited me on my return home. I was under contract to the BBC with crucial writing deadlines to meet. Of course I could have pleaded my bereavement and I'm sure there would have been understanding, but somehow I knew if I backed out, I'd be turning away avenues of opportunity that might provide some solution to my future.

A year before, my producer Polly Thomas and I had pitched an original idea for a drama series to the BBC. This would be a history of Britain in the twentieth century to be told in the unpublished diaries, letters and memoirs of ordinary people from all walks of life. Covering a decade at a time under the title of 'Writing the Century', these were to be broadcast on *Woman's Hour* in weekly tranches a few months apart. The major challenge in the beginning had been finding unpublished material that went back as far as 1900: a search that had already taken me, months before, to research libraries and archives up and down the country; but back then I would come home to discuss it all with Jim. Now I was on my own and faced with delivery dates for four weeks of broadcasts and twenty scripts already scheduled for that year. Friends and family were concerned that the size of the task would prove too difficult in the circumstances but in retrospect I now think having that purpose helped me to structure a way through the chaos. Each day I had to get up, go to my desk and work for hour after hour. My immediate circle of friends left me alone at my request. I had few phone calls and few visitors and in my necessary withdrawal from the world there was a kind of protection that enabled me to heal a little. One evening I came in to find a message on my answering machine from the rabbi at the synagogue, Ian Morris, who had only just heard of Jim's death and not from me; my involvement there remained very spasmodic and infrequent. Several times, since nominally joining after my mother's death, I had told Jim I was resigning my membership. I wasn't leading an authentic Jewish life I said. Jim wisely told me I didn't need to do anything drastic and that I shouldn't burn my boats as one day I 'might need the synagogue'. Now Ian Morris was asking if he could help and would I like to come to see him and I said, 'Yes.'

We sat in the darkened foyer and drank mugs of tea he had

brewed; no one else was there and, in his kindness and his own more reflective personality, I found myself able to talk freely. He had no golden panacea to remove the real and imagined doubts I had about being forever on the outside, but intellectually he understood and made some comments. I have never been religious. What I was seeking was my own community and what he gently pointed out was that if I wanted it enough I needed to reach out and become more actively involved instead of waiting on the touchlines to be invited in. With some apprehension I began to take more part in communal activities and made several new friends. The welcome was warm and inclusive but I could not excuse myself from envying others their unthinking confidence in both themselves and their birthright. So be it. Time was not infinite as I cruelly now knew. Whatever the anomalies were, they were my anomalies and not shared by all the progeny of converts. Either I was in or I was out, and I chose to be in.

Gradually the raw grief of Jim's death was replaced by a deep mourning for everything we had had in our life together. It was up to me to accept that my own life would now go on without him and to put some value into my future. I tried a gym and didn't like it. I tried a rumba class and nearly passed out. I went walking in the Dales and saw my first ever kingfisher. My gas cooker blew up on me as I was cooking and I coped. Then one night of teeming rain, Maureen, a friend, took me to the theatre in Harrogate to see a performance of Matthew Bourne's all male *Swan Lake*. It was still pouring down when we came out and she kindly told me she would bring the car round from the car park; there was no point in both of us getting wet. I'd taken little notice of her car when she collected me, other than that it was black and largish and my eyesight at night was always problematic. When a black car pulled up outside the theatre, I made a dash for it with my head down, yanked open the car door and thankfully hurled myself inside. 'Oh, that was so kind of you,' I said. 'You must be soaked.' Only to hear a clipped voice besides me say, in the unmistakable tones of North Yorkshire entitlement, 'Do you mind! I am waiting for my wife. Will you please get out of this car?' I turned to look at the elderly white-haired gentleman besides me and started laughing. I was still laughing as I got out. I stood on the pavement, still unable to see properly, which involved me stepping forwards to each car that stopped and calling through its window, 'Excuse me. Are you, Maureen?' in case I made the same mistake again. But I was laughing: I was laughing again.

Chapter 14

'WRITING THE CENTURY'

I had written a play called *Modelling Spitfires* a few years earlier for myself and the brilliant actor, Chris Wilkinson, a co-founder with me of Yellow Leaf Theatre; now it was going into the New End Theatre in Hampstead for a three-week run with Julie Higginson giving a lovely performance in the third part. Ironically, although not overtly stated, it was about a middle-aged brother and sister in a Jewish family and I stayed throughout the run in a guest house in Golders Green, which nicely underlined the provenance of the piece.

It was during the run of this play that I met Nigel, a Scot, down from the Borders to stay with his actress daughter, Lindesay, who had brought him to see the show at a Saturday matinee. From prior correspondence, she knew she'd be meeting up there with my agent, Patricia, and was hoping Patricia might take her on as a client. Afterwards the four of us had tea together and while Patricia and Lindesay talked, I found myself in conversation with this engaging man. For the first time since Jim's death I was having a proper conversation about theatre, music, ideas. I did not know at this point that I'd met another political animal, only this time it was Scottish Independence not youthful Marxism that drove him. Probably just as well. I seemed to attract political men who took it as a given that I ate the *Guardian* for breakfast when all I ever was, and am, as Jim always used to say, is 'a tummy socialist'. In that first meeting I did learn that Nigel, like me, was widowed, and a retired professor of history and that both his parents had been Scottish actors. As our tea interlude was coming to a close, Patricia concluded her professional conversation with Lindesay on the other side of the table, and turned up her charms, full-beam on this attractive man. Rather grumpily I left her the field and went off to prepare for the evening show. But later in the evening I had a text from Nigel suggesting I might like an outing away from the big smoke the following day, a Sunday and my free day.

We went to Leeds Castle which I had never visited before and I was on best behaviour. I think I'd forgotten entirely how to be in the exclusive company of one man and started talking nonsense. At one point I said in confident tones as we walked the grounds, 'I don't know about you, Nigel, but I am a Royalist.' It wasn't so much that these were decidedly not his views, as I later learned, but that for some reason I thought playing the entitled Tory lady would earn me 'brownie points'. Nigel dealt graciously with this one, probably by telling me he'd expel the lot of them (mild for him) and I relaxed. His actor parents had worked a lot for BBC Scotland and he had grown up speaking BBC English, which, as he said, was a formative experience if you went to an old grammar school in the Gorbals talking as he did and with a name like Nigel. Invariably he was challenged anywhere in England and also in Europe when he said he was a Scot with the rejoinder, delivered almost aggressively, 'Well, you don't sound it.' On planes, trains and ferries there was always someone. At Leeds Castle that day, I think I was trying to place exactly who and what he was and fit in with that but I ended up sounding like my mother, and now blush at the memory though it didn't spoil a lovely day. We ended up driving back to Hampstead to have dinner together in The Wells Tavern, where we talked and talked until gone eleven o'clock. Easter was coming up. Nigel told me he would be setting off shortly to drive to his house in Italy. He and his late wife, Jean, both passionate Italophiles, had planned to live their retirement as six months in Italy and six months in Scotland when her death cruelly cut short their dream. She had died in Italy just as all the renovations were finally completed on the apartment they had bought in a seventeenth-century palazzo in Pergola in Le Marche, but even in her sad absence the dream still held for Nigel. Impulsively that night, just as they were about to close, he asked if I would like to come out to Italy for some weeks that summer and just as impulsively I said, 'Yes.' Instinctively I knew he was a kind and honourable man, as well as many other interesting things, but more than that I had already thrown my bonnet over the rainbow in the last twenty-four hours, and he had done the same.

In the event I did the drive out to Italy with him that April on my first three-week visit, stopping off in Bouriege in South West France to stay with lifelong Scottish friends of his, Moira and Cameron, who made me very welcome. This had been the country of the Cathars of whose philosophy and beliefs I knew little until this point, and I liked the sound of them more and more. They were the persistent religious outsiders in Catholic Languedoc which made them my kind of people and I was curious to see more of what remained of them. The only drawback was that their strongholds were built defensively on high ground and I have always had a fear of heights. I was forced to confess this to Nigel when he proposed an assault on Montsegur, the highest of them all. 'No,' I said, 'no, no! I can't go up there. I simply refuse.' He was very kind but firm, treating me as a semi-hysteric who needed taking in hand, which somehow got me up the Pic's perilous track to the castle and then beyond that on a further climb inside to stand triumphantly in the castle's gateway arch, the Pyrenees behind me. I was so proud of myself I danced on the spot. 'Look at me. I've done it all by myself.' (Not true.) 'Aren't I clever.' We climbed two more castles and I even finished on the roof of the tower of Puivert.

After South West France we made our way south to Menton to pick up a coastal route, finally crossing into Italy by the Colle Alto to arrive in the Piedmont city of Cuneo with its enormous central piazza. The next day we went on to Vicenza where every street corner and square was a feast of Palladian architecture topped off by the exquisite Teatro Olimpico; the first perfectly preserved sixteenth-century theatre I had ever seen. Our final stop off before Le Marche was in Arqua at Petrarch's house. Here in those quiet gardens scented with box hedge was an idyll of contentment and beauty. From the airy loggia Petrarch might have sat to write his sonnets to Laura with the vista of the Eugenian Hills stretched out in front of him. I was entranced. The whole trip that first spring was magic to me. We talked non-stop all the way finding more and more coincidences in our lives, including Nigel's connection to the history department of Leeds University and to two men in particular, one of whom, Nicholas Pronay, was a close friend of Jim's, and, as it turned out, of Nigel's too.

Until this point my knowledge of Italy was limited to Venice, Rome, Positano and Taormina in Sicily but over several summers, my knowledge and love of the country increased as I came to know the Italian way of life. The little hilltop city of Pergola, close to Senigallia on the Adriatic coast, is set in rich agricultural land supporting vines, cherries, olive groves and crops. Greener than

Tuscany or neighbouring Umbria, it is characterised by valleys and ridges running down to the sea twenty miles away. As a working town off the beaten track it has escaped obvious tourist incursions. Modern buildings on the outskirts conceal, behind city walls, a *centro storico* with old buildings and Renaissance palaces. Over time this authenticity had attracted some Dutch and English couples to make the area into their permanent home. As we became friendly with them and also met and made Italian friends, we found ourselves part of a lively social scene that took to the streets and squares in the summer months with *festas* and saints' days and any other excuse for a party. But above all it was the beauty of the Palazzo Badalucchi itself that sealed the whole experience. Now divided into six apartments, with high ceilings and frescoed walls, it had originally been built, at some time before 1680, for the Badalucchi family, whose coat of arms was carved above the heavy double doors that gave off the street. Once inside, an arched cobbled carriageway led to the carriage houses at the back of the Palazzo, from where a garden, now heavily overgrown, sloped down to the Cesano River. An impressive stone staircase led up to the elegant *piano nobile* with its long covered loggia overlooking the garden and then continued to a second floor of three apartments. Here, in the largest one, Jean and Nigel had made their second home, restoring the frescoed ceilings in the three reception rooms with exquisite attention to detail. In contrast to the public rooms, the kitchen, bathroom and bedrooms had been modernised for comfort and the whole refurbishment completed with the renovation of the wide terrace leading off from the kitchen where oleanders and a rose bush thrived. From June onwards we ate most of our meals out there as the swallows ducked and weaved in the evenings and the bells from the adjacent twelfth-century Duomo rang out the angelus. Perfection.

Here Nigel stayed from May to September in absolute content and here I spent a large part of each summer too with gaps in between back home to catch up with the grandchildren or work commitments. I became adept, and inured, to flying out of Stansted courtesy of Ryanair to Ancona where Nigel would meet me and the long summer would continue, usually with at least one visit to the open air opera house in Macerata further south in Le Marche.

Like most people picking up a language later in life I understood more Italian than I had confidence to speak. I would sit in the hairdresser's on the Corso in Pergola where Ophelia, having warmly greeted me, would explain me away to the Italian matrons who were always in there as permanent fixtures with, 'Don't worry she's English and she doesn't understand a word. She lives in Palazzo Badalucchi with that man from Scotland with the blue car who had Davide from Senigalia to repaint their frescoes. He's a *professore* and his wife died'. 'Ah, *il Scozzese di Badalucchi*,' they would all say and nod their heads and smile in my direction and I'd smile back. They, like all Pergolese, were a delight to me.

Logistically in the beginning there were challenges; between us there were three homes – in Scotland, Yorkshire and Italy. At first our comings and goings between the places were complicated but autumns were in Leeds and marked the beginning of Nigel's introduction to the North Yorkshire dales and the North Yorkshire coast line. After Christmas, I joined Nigel in the Borders for Hogmanay and Burns Nights.

In a mirror image of my Italian experience I quickly saw how little I really knew of Scotland starting with the Borders themselves where he had his home. Overlooked by many in their haste to get to what they consider 'the real Scotland', the lovely Tweed valley around Peebles and Melrose is a surprise and a delight with Edinburgh barely thirty miles away on a cross-country route that starts in the rolling landscape of the Moorfoot Hills. Further afield Nigel introduced me to the Fife and Ayrshire coasts and then the Highlands. Mull and Skye were firsts for me, passing over Rannoch Moor and through the Great Glen to catch the ferry at Mallaig. In many ways, seen like this, Scotland became as exotic as Italy to me and viewed through the eyes of a passionate Scot who had been pro-independence since he was a student, I gained an insight into a national pride I had little understood before. Nigel's years away from Scotland, spent with his professional career in England, had been a kind of exile from his country and his culture. I knew all about not quite fitting in to your surroundings, whether tangibly as in his case, or metaphorically as in mine. It made for a shared understanding between us.

If Yorkshire, Scotland and Italy were autumn, winter and summer, it left early spring as the ideal time to explore other places. One thing we were in complete agreement over was that neither of us fancied long haul flights anymore; then we promptly went to New York as our first flying trip together.

Catriona, Nigel's elder daughter, a diplomat who worked in the Foreign Office, had been posted to the British Embassy to the UN in New York. Provided with a wonderful apartment on the Upper East Side, hers was an invitation not to miss. Nigel hadn't been back to America since his chair, teaching at Dartmouth College, New Hampshire, and although he continued to teach the college's London programme for twenty-five years, for one reason or another he had not returned since the late eighties. I'd not been back to NY since Nerissa left in 1996. Now, it seemed like another era: 9/11 had changed something irrevocably. There was the same sense of hurry, the same mass of people on the sidewalks, the same sense of scale but something upbeat had gone. Some of the New Yorkers' optimism and wise-cracking had been replaced by a kind of weariness and a dogged determination to carry on as normal. For the first time Manhattan wasn't chipper. Shades of my early childhood in bombed out Manchester came back to me. Perhaps, just like my home city after the war, it would need a couple of decades to recover from one of the greatest air raids imaginable. There were some happy days of course, walking across Brooklyn Bridge to stop and look down on the East River; a boat trip round the whole of Manhattan Island; visits to the Met and The Frick Collection; a joyous production of *The Pyjama Game* off Broadway and a very memorable private tour round the UN building organised by Catriona – but NY wasn't a city for a rest cure and in subsequent spring breaks we sought the Mediterranean in Crete, Malta, Toledo, Seville and Lisbon. The one exception was when Nigel came with me on my second visit to Bialystok.

Not only came with me but initiated the visit. He wanted to share what my roots in the country meant to me and as we walked the streets in the snow that came down that late March, he was staggered by how little was left of the city's rich Jewish past and as a historian, profoundly shocked. Once, proportionately, the largest Jewish city in Europe with nearly two thirds of the population Jewish for over a hundred years, there was now nothing. Plaque after plaque conscientiously reminded one that here was once a Jewish synagogue, school, ambulance service, maternity hospital, theatre, press. It became overwhelming in its sadness. Only in the elegance of the Branicki Palace gardens, now the home of the medical school of Bialystok University, was there a trace of the older city. Ironically this was where the Jewish history in Bialystok had begun when the enlightened Count Jan Branicki had granted full legal privileges to Jews in the early eighteenth century. The palace, built in a French style with its complex of pavilions and sculptures, still stood intact but the community that it had presided over had vanished; just eleven Jews now lived in Bialystok. We'd had enough. In a conscious effort to take away a more positive image from our Polish trip we decided to drive out to the Bialowieza National Park at the end of the week to see some bison. The two hour drive was fairly straightforward, winding through village after village where giant storks nested on the telegraph poles like some drawings out of Hans Christian Andersen. In the town of Hajnowka we stopped for a coffee in a shopping mall and were served by an intense-looking young man who spoke good English. He had immediately spotted Nigel's Scottish independence YES badge and was well-informed about the whole independence movement. Here was another political animal called Christophe. He had a brother at Glasgow University he said and was himself working for his PhD at Warsaw University. Then turning to me, he correctly guessed I was on a visit to find Jewish ancestors. Where did I come from in England he asked. 'Leeds,' I said. 'Ah, then do you know Zygmunt Bauman?' and, preposterously, I did. 'Zyggy' Bauman had held the chair of Sociology at Leeds University for twenty-five years and was internationally known as a sociologist and philosopher who had died the previous year at the age of ninety-one. It was the most remarkable coincidence and somehow reaffirming that a Polish Jewish scholar of such eminence as Zygmunt Bauman, forced to give up his Polish citizenship in 1968 amidst a new wave of anti-Semitism, should be revered and respected by a young man in present-day Poland. This was a good memory to carry away from the trip, also the basis of my continuing email friendship with Christophe. And we did manage to see some bison that day as well.

Gradually we worked out our own pattern of a shared life with our four daughters very much in the forefront. For a while my grandsons didn't know quite what to make of Nigel. Robbie later confessed that early on he thought Nigel was a carpet fitter because he had a brown suede gilet with many pockets in it, just like the man who had come to fit the new carpets in their house in Sunninghill. Between the four daughters there were seven grandsons eventually, dotted between Sunninghill and Crystal Palace and Matlock, where Nerissa and Adam had a beautiful old farmhouse set above the Amber valley. Over the summers most of our two families were able to come out on visits to Pergola and the children loved getting down to the beach in Marotta or eating out in a hillside trattoria. Some people found a recital of our itineraries of comings and goings exhausting but somehow we adapted to it and in any case if I was working that changed all plans.

Out of the publicity garnered when the broadcasts of 'Writing the Century' went out, I was invited to become writer in residence at King's College, London. The brief was to look into the cache of colonial nurses' letters held in the Bodleian Library in Oxford to see if there was enough material there to create an original drama both for a university-rehearsed reading and eventually for a further week of 'Writing the Century' on *Woman's Hour*. For a year I was in possession of a Bodleian Reader's ticket and relished the experience of coming and going and of sharing the experience of my own sample of academe with Nigel, just as I would have shared it with Jim, who would have been tickled pink for me. The Colonial Nursing Association was set up in 1895 as a means of supplying the British colonies and dominions with trained professional nurses who could look after the health of white colonists abroad. In the beginning my research yielded little. So many of the letters, written home to the secretary of the CNA, read like the dutiful epistles one might write to one's headmistress, such as 'Arrived here safely to no alarms and received a warm welcome'; and 'My camel ride into Khartoum was very pleasant'; or 'Two of us are sharing a room and have a delightful house boy to cook for us.' This was another world in which would-be colonial nurses were advised to have, at least, one cocktail dress and one full evening gown in their luggage. I did eventually find something meatier in the 1920s with an intrepid nurse based in Newfoundland who served a vast area that was icebound for three months of the year, leaving her to cope with every eventuality as the nearest doctor was twenty miles away in Burin. I contrasted her life with a nurse in Mauritius who had sought the service out of economic necessity after her fiancé was killed in the First World War. This was the case with so many of the nurses of this generation: their expectations of the life they thought they'd have snuffed out in Northern France and I came to admire their courage and lack of self-pity in letter after letter.

What both the women I'd chosen to focus on had in common was that they were outsiders in the communities in which they lived. I had a homing instinct for such personalities. Straight away I was in a territory I could relate to.

For Week 15 of 'Writing the Century' I had come across another such woman called Catherine Thackray, who kept a diary for the last five years of her life as she battled, bravely, with breast cancer. Born in 1922, and married to a Huddersfield solicitor, Catherine had had several different careers since her graduation from the London School of Economics before ending up as a secondary modern schoolteacher while also serving as a local magistrate. Politics and political engagement were a large part of her life. She was an early member of the Fabian Society and the local secretary for CND. In 1984 she went to Greenham Common to take part in the active protest around the perimeter's base for which she was arrested, leading to her removal from the bench. The diaries consistently reflect her strong views and wide, liberal sympathies. As a Southerner transported to life in the North on her marriage to a Quaker pacifist, she had little in common with the society of successful business people she found herself among but 'earned international fame and the admiration of many for her passionate belief in many causes' – to quote from her *Guardian* obituary.

The amount of material I had at my disposal was considerable and there was so much of her story I wanted to tell in the five episodes of *Woman's Hour* that would make up the week. I timed each episode rigorously, as was my practice, by reading it out loud over and over again and cutting sentences ruthlessly here and there to bring it in at exactly the 14 minutes 20 seconds required. I was quite proud of myself for this. But I had reckoned without the marvellous Eleanor Bron, and the marvellous Eleanor Bron voice in the role of Catherine.

As I sat in the recording studio and heard her read the first lines my spirits sank. 'I have decided to keep a diary,' Catherine Thackray begins, only what I heard was 'I ha-ve…de-ci-ded…to… kee-p…a…di-ary.' That inimical, languorous voice was off; so was all my timing from start to finish. I was delighted to have her excellent performance but sorry for the amount of script that ended up on the cutting room floor. I had to lose quite a lot of lines I was keen on, but the compensation was that her distinctive delivery brought an edge to Catherine. Here was a Southern voice amongst the Northern vowels of her husband and family that truly heightened the sense of a woman who walked alone.

Now, in a short space of time, I was fortunate to work with two wonderful actresses with distinctive voices; both happened to be Jewish – Eleanor Bron and Miriam Margolyes. Miriam played the Jewish matriarch in my dramatisation of Lennard Davis's book, *Shall I Say A Kiss* which deals with the courtship and marriage of his profoundly deaf parents, as they sought to emigrate to America. Her performance was vibrant, warm and funny and devoid of any of the stereotypical memes a lesser talent might have drawn on.

Facing the quota system of the American immigration authority was daunting for the young couple. They had two strikes against them: for being deaf and being Jewish in the America of the 1930s, which saw an increase in anti-Semitism. Playing them we had two young deaf actors whose performances were immeasurably enhanced by having Miriam Margolyes's generous support and encouragement throughout, all achieved without a trace of patronisation.

By coincidence I had a personal connection with Miriam Margolyes. This was through a close friend of mine, Susie Robinson, whom I had first met through Hampstead Labour Party in the mid-sixties. Some years later she had returned to live in Glasgow, her home city. At a Jewish genealogical forum there sometime in the late nineties she had met Miriam who was in Glasgow researching, I believe, her father's family, in the city in which he had grown up. Miriam and Susie hit it off at once in a way that didn't surprise me at all. Both were terrific life forces, large personalities in whose company one would always feel better. Both, like me too, had fathers who were doctors. I never found out if Miriam's father and Susie's father might have trained in Glasgow around the same time, but I did know that Susie had kept in touch with Miriam and liked her a lot. Susie, a single parent with a grown-up son, had had many different careers after training as a nurse at Guy's Hospital and now ran a wacky antique shop in the West End of Glasgow called 'All Our Yesterdays'. There she presided daily in her colourful kaftans and navy blue nail polish. In its back room she also practised as a healer working with crystals that stood about the place in great stalagmites of rose quartz and amethyst. Sadly, I now had to tell Miriam that Susie had died three years previously of lung cancer. Miriam was extremely sorry to hear this and her warmth to me over the loss of an important friend was very touching. As we say in the North, 'she has no side': truly the greatest compliment.

Chapter 15

A NEW END

Rather as a last hurrah, I had decided to take something once more to the Edinburgh Fringe Festival with Yellow Leaf Theatre. The Fringe had become gargantuan even since the last time I was there in the early nineties. At any hour of the day, evening or late into the night, there were now thousands of shows competing for audiences. Comedy and comedians featured heavily along with cabaret. A serious theatre piece, facing 150 other dramas even in its own ninety-minute slot, was swimming against the tide but, with a small Arts Council grant, I felt it was worth a try.

The idea had been simmering for some time. As far back as the 1980s I had come across the work of the *kindertransport* poet, Karen Gershon, who was published by both Faber and Gollancz. Born in Bielefeld, Westphalia, in 1923, she was on one of the first *kindertransports* to Britain as a fifteen-year-old girl, leaving behind her parents who later perished at the Salaspils concentration camp, near Riga. Her poetry, all written in her adopted language, and at one point linked in a *Guardian* review with the work of such poets as Seamus Heaney, tells almost exclusively of the impact of the Holocaust on her life and, though she went on to marry and have four children, she was never really reconciled to a new country and to exile. Her most famous poem, at one time included in a GCSE syllabus, was about the fate of her parents; its opening lines ran:

> The morning they set out from home
> I was not there to comfort them...
>
> Both my parents died in camps
> I was not there to comfort them
> I was not there they were alone
> My mind refuses to conceive the life
> The death they must have known

Telling her story as a one-woman show remained an elusive idea to me that I couldn't nail until I came across the fact that in 1990, three years before she died, Channel 4 had taken Karen Gershon back to Bielefeld to make a documentary about her life. My play, *Karen's Way: A Kindertransport Life*, took shape from the idea of her returning to her hometown for the first time since she left in 1939. I set the action on the eve of filming, with Karen wandering through the park in Bielefeld when, out of the shadows, steps her fifteen-year-old self, dressed in a German school uniform of the 1930s. Delighted, astonished at the reunion, Older and Younger Karen together remember, laugh, dance, weep and sing. With permissions from the Gershon family and working closely with her daughter, the artist, Stella Tripp, many lines of the poems came out almost conversationally in the dialogue. On arrival in Britain Karen Gershon was first sent to a reception camp in Kent and from there to Scotland, Wales, Bradford and Leeds in a series of jobs that included work in a department store, a textile mill and the chorus line of a third-rate touring pantomime company. All the time her one obsession was to master the language sufficiently to begin writing her first poems in English. Again I was using music to evoke and enlarge the dramatic moments in the play and again David Riley and Marion Raper were with me, superbly playing everything from Bach and Shostakovich to Benjamin Britten and Noel Gay's 'Lambeth Walk'. I had written the part of the young schoolgirl for Nigel's daughter, Lindesay, hoping it might give her the break that every young actor needs. She had exactly the right kind of quixotic intelligence and distinctiveness that ensured the tragic elements in the play never became sentimental and we made a good stage team.

The show received very good reviews and some memorable audience reactions. At one performance an elderly American man, himself a *kindertransport* survivor, told me that during the play, in the darkened space of the venue, he had wept for the first time. Another woman got to her feet to give us a standing ovation, rousing the rest of the audience to join her. We had healthy-sized audiences too in part due to Nigel's tireless daily campaign to recruit the punters. He had pitched himself into the whole thing with such enthusiasm and invaluable practical help that we all came to rely on him more and more as a kind of general company manager. I think he enjoyed it, and like Jim all those years before, he stood daily at the junction of The Mound and the Royal Mile handing out flyers and enthusing about the play, wearing the company sweatshirts he'd insisted we should all don for publicity purposes. Designed by him, these had the name of the play – *Karen's Way: A Kindertransport Life* – printed on the front together with the venue details and times of the performances. One afternoon, two Glasgow couples, fresh from the Tattoo, came bubbling down towards him from the Lawnmarket, when one of the men spotted his sweatshirt and called out, 'Aw naw! No Karen's wey again! It's bin Karen's wey fir ten years. Is it naw time it wis Sandy's?'

The atmosphere of the Fringe was like perpetual carnival time and infectious but it had become increasingly a young people's game. Having a late meal with Nigel one evening after a performance, I received a text message from one of the Festival promoters asking me if I was going out that evening: the time was 11.45 p.m.

One outcome of the whole thing was that we were invited to perform the play the following spring in Jerusalem. I had not been back to Israel for over ten years; the last time was with Jim and I wondered how I'd feel. Our trip then had taken us from Upper Galilee and Lake Tiberias in the North down to Eilat near the Egyptian border. Jim had been fascinated by the country and by everything it had achieved. For him the greatest conundrum was Jerusalem: why had one square mile in the entire world seen the birthplace of three of the world's major religions, Judaism, Christianity and Islam. So many impressions crowd in on a first visit with perhaps the greatest being the sudden reality that locations mentioned in the Old and New Testaments are actual places on the ground, not myths. Jim's astonishment at it all was a source of great pleasure for me and the memory of that time was still fresh; would returning be tricky for me?

I needn't have worried, for though our schedule was hectic, in what spare time there was I was able to share the beauty of Jerusalem with Nigel and delighted to see it exert its strange power on him too. The most remarkable aspect of the warm reception the play received came from Karen Gershon's daughter, Naomi, and Naomi's sons. One of the deepest ironies of Karen's life was that she had always dreamed of living in Israel and never did for any length of time, but three of her four children had made their lives there. Naomi's sons, now young men in their early twenties, remembered their grandmother well and when they told me they forgot entirely for the length of the performance that I was not her up there on the stage and that the play had honoured her, I felt I had achieved what I set out to do.

Over a couple of days I came to know and appreciate Naomi. On the Friday evening she invited us to join her for a *shabbat* meal. We sat on the terrace of her house drinking coffee and watching the light fade from the Judaean hills in the distance. The mixed marriage between her English father and Jewish mother had left her with different, but similar, confusions to myself about identity. Unlike me, she had not been brought up in the Jewish faith though with a strong awareness of her Jewish inheritance and of her mother's upbringing in a loving Jewish family in Germany. When first Naomi's two elder brothers, and then she herself, ended up living in Israel it caused division between her parents. Her father was unprepared for what he saw as their choice of their mother's identity over his. He thought that he and Karen had together created a loving family in which sectarianism had been abolished in the aftermath of her traumatic experience. Naomi had never intended to make her life in Israel. Her post-university visit to the country had been intended as just that, a visit, but she had fallen in love with an Ethiopian Jew and settled there to raise her family.

There were layers upon layers here. The plight of the Ethiopian Jews in Israel had been a painful battle to gain recognition of their right to call themselves Jewish. Believed to be descendants of the lost Hebrew tribe of Dan from 586 BC, they had been completely isolated for centuries from Jewish communities in other parts of the world but when they arrived in Israel, after appalling persecution in their own country and dangerous journeys through the Sudan, they faced discrimination and racism. Exile and loss, whether real or metaphorical, touched my story and that of Naomi and of her husband, Abren. In her husband's case the exile was from his childhood in Ethiopia as well as from full acceptance into Israel; in Naomi's it was exile from her father and in my case it was self-imposed exile on myself through 'thinking too finely on a point'.

Between Edinburgh in the summer and Israel the following spring, I had moved house, nearly five years after Jim's death.

For the first three years, the idea of putting the family home on the market after forty-two years of living there was anathema to me. I wrapped it round myself for comfort, wandering from room to room and nodding my head in satisfaction. I lived in the large kitchen and my bedroom and kept the rest just as it had always been, shouting down the friends who suggested that perhaps it was now too big for me. No. No. I wouldn't hear of that. Then one winter night, I was dropped off by taxi from an evening out, and stood at the top of the long drive looking down on the house and thought, this is mad. Why am I struggling to maintain all this? The large garden alone was too much for me. I worried about keeping the place warm in winter; it needed a new boiler, a new drive in a couple of years. Every three years the exterior needed re-painting which involved scaffolding. Instead of the balm it had brought me in the beginning, now I was on the edge of anxiety about the place. In that moment as I stood there my decision was swift and definite: it was time to move.

Selling it and finding the right place took two years with a few collapsed sales in between but eventually I found a completely different kind of house in the same neighbourhood. Situated at the top of a cul-de-sac, overlooking conservation land behind a dry stone wall, it had a large open plan downstairs like a studio space and room enough to put the family up on visits. Nigel, who had missed a calling as an architect, came up with a fireplace idea that gave the whole thing a focal point and also designed the Indian stone terrace which faced the tall trees in the conservation land where owls hooted at night. After four decades of living in a house off the main road, the peace and evening stillness gave off a deep content.

Chapter 16

AND NOW

Almost like a sign that the same life would simply continue in another place, soon after moving in I found myself back working at Leeds Playhouse in an Alan Bennett double bill to celebrate the playwright's eightieth birthday.

Leeds recognises Alan Bennett as her special son. Loved by the whole country, Leeds is enormously proud to claim him as her very own. He holds a mirror up to its people and gives them back to themselves with affection and understanding. So much of his writing takes inspiration from his growing up in the city and from his Yorkshire roots. Behind the brilliance of his wry self-deprecation is a superb craftsman and a clever man who might have had a different career as a history don at Oxford.

My last time at Leeds, I'd played Alan Bennett's Mum in *Lady in The Van*; this time I was there to play Mrs Clegg in *Enjoy* in the Quarry Theatre there (a part I'd played in Manchester a few years previously) and Irene Ruddock in 'Lady of Letters', one of the monologues in his *Talking Heads* series that are so well known from television. Both these shows were directed by James Brining in immaculate productions of great flair and imagination. In *Enjoy* he used live video to amplify and enhance key moments to brilliant and original comic effect. In *Talking Heads* he balanced the comic alongside moments of aching poignancy.

Working on a script written by such a master as Alan Bennett is a joy. Every single word is there for a purpose. Character, attitude, social standing and characters' relationship to the world around them are all conveyed with apparent artlessness.

Irene Ruddock in 'Lady of Letters' writes spiteful letters and stirs up trouble because she is lonely and wants attention. Acutely aware of a world pecking order, she is a snob and a passive racist. In the end she goes too far and, after repeated warnings, ends up in prison where her life changes dramatically. In prison she finds companionship, inclusion and purpose. She joins a literary appreciation class, a dressmaking class and a bookbinding class as well as becoming a star pupil on a commercial course. By the end of the monologue her life is transformed and as she says, 'I'm so *happy*.'

Before opening in the Courtyard Theatre, the second auditoria of Leeds Playhouse, the production, which consisted of three separate Bennett monologues to make up a full evening's programme, was going out into the community. James Brining had only been appointed as Artistic Director two years previously but he was Leeds born and bred which gave him a particular insight into Alan Bennett's work and a strong connection to the city. He felt keenly that the theatre belonged to the whole of the city, not just the middle classes of North Leeds who could afford the ticket prices. One of the early things he had done was to appoint ambassadors of the theatre whose role was to build bridges between the community and the theatre. In social clubs and leisure centres, relationships were gradually being cemented. New faces were appearing at 'Heydays', the Playhouse's flagship creative programme for the over fifty-fives, where older people could develop creative skills and meet others. Preview tickets were offered at a token price to encourage a new audience across the threshold. In this same spirit of goodwill, James had come up with another initiative for the Alan Bennett monologues. Aided by the local evening paper he announced there would be a free performance of a *Talking Heads* monologue in every single one of the Leeds city post codes, from mansions to flats, in private homes and community centres, for friends and family. No place was debarred unless it couldn't provide a chair and a square of space for the actor to sit or stand in. It was a case of hurry, hurry to be first in your postal area to apply.

From the beginning I relished the fun of a scheme that gave me some very memorable evenings. Arriving early at the chosen address with a member of the technical team to check the general layout, I would be warmly greeted by the host, then shown to a bedroom where I could change. My very first performance was in a South Leeds house back-to-back with a tiny living room almost completely taken over by a large leather sofa. Five people were squashed on to it with others perched on the sofa arms or standing by the door. I squeezed my way in past an Alsatian dog that sniffed at my skirt and stepped over a toddler sprawled on the floor. When I sat on my designated chair, my knees touched the knees of the woman nearest me on the sofa. Throughout the forty minutes of the monologue I was making direct, intimate eye contact with all of them. When they laughed it felt like a party. At one point the Alsatian decided to be friends and came and put his head in my lap so I patted him and kept going. They loved that and their rapt attention reminded me that all theatre is just telling stories to our tribe, in different cultures across the world, as we have done since time immemorial. Afterwards I joined them all for a drink. Any shyness was immediately dispersed because the artificial barrier between performer and audience hadn't existed. Two of them told me they'd never been to the theatre except to 'pantomimes when I was a kiddie'. We talked about the most ordinary things, our families, how I learned my lines (a perennial one), had I ever been on television? I told them about the cheap preview tickets and they promised they would 'give it a go'. It felt like the most worthwhile thing to be doing and afterwards I was on a high.

Not all venues were equally successful. My monologue was the only one of the three that required a quick change of costume into the 'prison' garb in my last scene and because of the configuration of some houses, I was reduced on one occasion to stepping through the French window into the garden and hunkering down behind a garden shed. On another occasion I confidently strode across the room, pulled open a door and nearly fell down the cellar steps. Each evening we returned to the theatre for a post-mortem with our fellow actors. Some of the post codes yielded large, detached houses and sitting rooms where twenty or more gathered for a performance to be followed afterwards by canapés and prosecco, but I had none of those and didn't mind a bit.

However, on the final Saturday I picked the short straw: a care home in the city centre an hour after lunchtime. Being the weekend, the manager was absent. Things were being run by some charming Filipino care assistants but as they wheeled in the residents, many of them semi-recumbent, I sensed a challenge. Within minutes several of them started snoring loudly and then the comments started, 'Is she going to sing?' 'Oh, I wish she'd stop!' And then, 'Shut-up. Shut-up. Shut-up!' and, 'I can't stand her', screeched from the back of the room by someone obviously in distress. By mistake I'd been booked into the dementia wing. The kindest thing would have been to stop and I would have done so except for a tiny, birdlike woman who sat near me at the front, hanging on to my every word. I've no idea who or what she thought I was but, as the lines came out, she started answering them.

'I'm just waiting for the evening paper. Not that there's much in it,' I said.

    'I know,' she said. *'Do you get it every night?'*

(At first I ignored her but then she dragged her chair nearer me.)

'The correspondence I initiated on the length of the Archbishop of Canterbury's hair seems to have gone off the boil,' I went on.

    'He should get it cut then shouldn't he,' said my new friend.

    'What's your name? I'm Margaret?'

(I looked to the stage manager I'd come with for some guidance; she shook her head, nonplussed.)

I ploughed on.

'Getting dark. The couple opposite just having their tea.'

    'Greedy pigs,' Margaret said.

    'They've just had their dinner. They'll get fat.'

And so it went on. Every time I hesitated she took my hands and shook them to urge me to continue. Somehow or other, in some surreal Samuel Beckett kind of duologue, she and I staggered through the whole thing to the end while the rest slept on. At the end of it all, the theatre photographer stepped up to take my photograph. He'd been following the community tour on its progress through the city to create a visual record. 'Wait,' I said. 'There were two of us in this performance' and I put my hand out to Margaret. 'Come on,' I said, 'you need to be in this picture.' I don't think even Christmas came anywhere near to it for her as I put my arm round her and told her to smile. Somewhere in the theatre to this day is a picture of Margaret and me performing in *Talking Heads*.

Initially, stepping out to do a dramatic monologue is daunting. You are absolutely on your own if things go wrong; there is no one else on stage to help you out. So often in rep one could rescue a fellow actor who had dried with the banal but necessary trick of saying, I suppose you were just about to tell me etcetera, etcetera and supplying their line in the hope of kick-starting them, like dealing with a rundown car battery. I've coped with actors late on stage, with a faulty tannoy system which somehow got crossed lines with a local taxi firm with original results, with props that don't work and animals that wee on stage. In the latter case it was an Irish Wolfhound chosen for its doleful expression that behaved beautifully for ten days, but once used to the whoops of audience delight at his first appearance, gradually became more and more at home. What do you do as dribbles of wee trickle down the stage towards the orchestra pit? I'd lost the contest by then: he was the star. Certain anxiety dreams seem fairly constant with actors. One is that all your teeth drop out on stage and you are scrabbling around on hands and knees trying to find them and shove them back in. Another is that you arrive on stage late, in the wrong costume and know you are the next to speak but you haven't a clue what play you are in, let alone what you should be saying. Although it gets a little irksome to be asked again and again, 'How do you remember all those lines?' it does get more challenging as you get older. A monologue or one woman show means it is just you for forty minutes, which is equivalent to knowing most of *Hamlet*. Initially, during *Talking Heads*, I had suggested I might have the script tucked away somewhere on stage but this was vetoed. I would never have needed it as it turned out but just knowing it was there might have given me given me confidence in the beginning. Once I got over the fear, I discovered it was exhilarating to have the space to myself. Here was autonomy and control. I liked it and followed it up by writing a one woman show for myself about the artist Nina Hamnett that was put on through Yellow Leaf Theatre and skilfully directed by the actress Jeannie Crowther, a good friend. It played in art galleries that showed Nina Hamnett's work, often alongside the actual painting the gallery owned, propped up on an easel beside me. I wanted to test my powers of memory and, if I'm honest, to ensure I kept working by creating work for myself. The profession isn't kind to older actresses; the parts get fewer; writers overlook us. There is a limit to how many grandmothers or old women are portrayed as having influence in the world, whereas male actors seem to go on and on. Lear; Prospero; Peer Gynt; Uncle Vanya, the list is long.

Roger Fry's portrait of Nina Hamnett, in the Stanley & Audrey Burton Gallery in Leeds, painted when they were lovers, was something I'd known and cared about long before the idea for a mono-drama about her took shape in my head. It captures Nina, aged twenty-four around 1914 with her success already established as the best-known woman artist in Paris at that time. Moving in a circle of friends and lovers that included Sickert, Pissaro, Epstein, Gaudier-Brzeska, Picasso and Modigliani she personified Bohemian Montparnasse. But by the 1950s she had squandered her great talent and, now an alcoholic, held court most days from a bar stool in the Wheatsheaf Tavern in Soho from where she could cadge the next drink. My one woman show called, '*Nina: Queen of Bohemia*', was intended to capture both her glory and her disintegration. Flamboyant, unpredictable, witty and kind, she was disowned by her very proper military family who, through the marriage of her sister

Helen to Catherine Booth's son, had ironic direct connections with the Salvation Army.

At the very first performance in Leeds I was surprised to see two small boys on the front row, flanked by their parents. They behaved impeccably throughout but I did wonder if the material was suitable for them. In my play Nina talks freely of her many lovers and of her attitudes to sex while getting steadily drunker and reciting bawdy limericks. After the show I received a message that someone would like to see me. I came front of house and met a young woman who was obviously the mother of the boys. She introduced herself to me as Nina Hamnett's great-niece, Emma Cartledge, and thanked me for the show and for the tribute it paid to her great-aunt of whom she knew little. Apparently Aunt Nina was rarely talked of by her father, Nina's nephew, and if she was at all, it was always as the black sheep of the family. Her great talent was barely mentioned. This was the first time Emma had realised to any degree the significance of Nina Hamnett's work and of her stature in the art world before alcoholism blighted her life. Emma thought her father might like to see the show to redeem the picture he carried of 'bad' Aunt Nina. She took away details of the tour dates but unhappily wrote to me later to say that her father had declined. I was saddened by this. As far as her family was concerned Nina Hamnett would, apparently, for ever be consigned to a bad press and destined to live on the margins, like Karen Gershon, though in a different way. Like me. The comparison, when it came to me, was suddenly obvious.

People like Nina Hamnett and Karen Gershon attracted me. I felt I could get inside their heads, just a little, after a lifetime of practice. Both women had enjoyed widespread critical approval, fame even in their time but both felt they never quite fitted in. Karen Gershon lived in perpetual exile and Nina Hamnett lived in the exile imposed on her by her disapproving family. Whilst my life story is different, there is one crucial thing that unites us: we are all outsiders.

I was never disowned by my family; I was never a refugee, but I still wait to be found out as an imposter. Not the full deal. More than anything, I envy those who are a hundred per cent sure of who they are. I have reached my seventies still carting round the same baggage and am resigned to the familiarity of it all. I still play the clown, the serious clown who hides behind the wide smile on their white face. Impossible to tell what's really going on in there, and I like it that way.

Out of the blue my Facebook page was hacked a year ago and amongst the many who emailed me to tell me about it, I received a phone call. The distinctive Northern voice said, 'You won't know who this is!' But I did. I knew instantly it was Paul. Someone, somewhere in the great Jewish diaspora since my return to the community must have given him my contact details. I had had no personal contact since that winter night en route to a school dance when I was seventeen years old. We chatted pleasantly for a while, filling in the broadest of outlines of our personal lives, our parents' lives and deaths, his career in alternative medicine, his marriage, the bar mitzvahs of his grandsons in the London synagogue he belonged to and concluded with one of those social promises to 'keep in touch'.

He had no idea of the significant role he'd played in my life on the crucial brink of adulthood. Without him I would have taken longer to realise that being on the outside looking inside is who I am and always have been from the beginning. It has shaped and formed me in all kinds of ways and both excuses and judges some of my behaviour. There must be a lot of us out there keeping our secrets. As long as we keep smiling, no one really knows the truth. I doubt that we even know it ourselves.

Acknowledgments

With many thanks to my partner, Nigel Mace, for all his unfailing support and for his help in digitally preparing my photographs for this book.

And with thanks to my editor at RedDoor Press, Heather Boisseau, for her skill and for making everything such a pleasure, to my proofreader Cathy Stagg, and most of all to my publisher, Clare Christian, for her encouragement from the beginning and for seeing this book through to publication along with the help of the dedicated team at RedDoor Press.

Find out more about RedDoor Press and sign up to our newsletter to hear about our **latest releases, author events,** exciting **competitions** and more at

reddoorpress.co.uk

YOU CAN ALSO FOLLOW US:

 @RedDoorBooks

 Facebook.com/RedDoorPress

 @RedDoorBooks